THE LIVING END

Queer Film Classics

Edited by Matthew Hays and Thomas Waugh

The enduring commercial success of LGBTQ2I films over recent generations offers proof of widespread interest in queer film within both pop culture and academia. Not only are recent works riding the wave of the new maturity of queer film culture, but a century of queer and proto-queer classics are in busy circulation thanks to a burgeoning online queer cinephile culture and have been brought back to life by omnipresent festivals and revivals. Meditations on individual films from queer perspectives are particularly urgent, unlocking new understandings of political as well as aesthetic and personal concerns.

Queer Film Classics at McGill-Queen's University Press emphasizes good writing, rigorous but accessible scholarship, and personal, reflective thinking about the significance of each film – writing that is true to the film, original, and enlightening and enjoyable for film buffs, scholars, and students alike. Books in the series are short – roughly 40,000 words – but well illustrated and allow for considerable depth. Exploring historical, authorial, and production contexts and drawing on filmic analysis, these open-ended essays also develop the author's personal interests or a subjective reading of the work's sexual identity discourses or reception. The series aims to meet the diversity, quality, and originality of classics in the queer film canon, broadly conceived, with equally compelling writing and critical insight. Books in the series have much to teach us, not only about the art of film but about the queer ways in which films can transmit our meanings, our stories, and our dreams.

THE LIVING END

Glyn Davis

McGill-Queen's University Press
Montreal & Kingston

ISBN 978-0-2280-2899-4 (paper)
ISBN 978-0-2280-2984-7 (ePDF)
ISBN 978-0-2280-2917-5 (ePUB)

Legal deposit third quarter 2026
Bibliothèque et Archives nationales du Québec

Printed in Canada on acid-free paper that is 100% ancient-forest-free, containing 100% sustainable, recycled fibre, and processed chlorine-free.

McGill-Queen's University Press in Montreal is on land which long served as a site of meeting and exchange amongst Indigenous Peoples, including the Haudenosaunee and Anishinabeg nations. In Kingston it is situated on the territory of the Haudenosaunee and Anishinaabek. We acknowledge and thank the diverse Indigenous Peoples whose footsteps have marked these territories on which peoples of the world now gather.

Library and Archives Canada Cataloguing in Publication

Title: The living end / Glyn Davis.
Names: Davis, Glyn (Reader in Screen Studies), author.
Series: Queer film classics (McGill-Queen's University Press)
Description: Series statement: Queer film classics | Includes bibliographical references and index.
Identifiers: Canadiana (print) 20260173045 | Canadiana (ebook) 20260173088 | ISBN 9780228028994 (softcover) | ISBN 9780228029847 (PDF) | ISBN 9780228029175 (EPUB)
Subjects: LCSH: Living end (Motion picture : 1992) | LCSH: Araki, Gregg—Criticism and interpretation. | LCSH: AIDS (Disease) in motion pictures. | LCSH: Gay people in motion pictures. | LCSH: Homosexuality in motion pictures.
Classification: LCC PN1997.L58 D38 2026 | DDC 791.43/72—dc23

This book was designed and typeset by studio oneonone in Minion 11/14.
Copyediting by Ryan Yates.

McGill-Queen's University Press
Suite 1720, 1010 Sherbrooke St West, Montreal, QC, H3A 2R7

Authorized safety representative in the EU: Mare Nostrum Group BV, Doelen 72, 4831 GR Breda, the Netherlands, gpsr@mare-nostrum.co.uk

Contents

Preface

Gregg Araki's third feature, *The Living End*, was released into cinemas in the United Kingdom on 12 February 1993. I had been eager to see the film since reading about it in the dossier on "New Queer Cinema" that appeared in the magazine *Sight and Sound* in September of the previous year. Subsequent reviews, positive or critical, only piqued my interest further. I was a second-year undergraduate at the University of Edinburgh at the time, and already an ardent cinephile; I would spend many pleasurable hours every week in the city's two arthouse cinemas, the Cameo and the Filmhouse, watching everything from new releases to late-night double bills of cult favourites.

The Living End was shown at the Filmhouse on 15, 16, and 17 March 1993. The screening I attended, at 5:15 p.m. on the Monday, was followed by an audience discussion. (I would love to reveal that the discussion forever changed my relationship to the film and contributed directly to the content of this book, but I remember nothing about it. Most likely, I failed to contribute and felt rather awkward.) That day in 1993 was an auspicious one for Edinburgh's queer film fans: a screening of *Orlando* (1992) at the Cameo featured a personal appearance by Tilda Swinton (I was unsuccessful in scoring a ticket for that one). In fact, other queer treats were also at the Filmhouse that week: *The Crying Game* (1992) and *Rebel Without a Cause* (1955).

The city's mainstream cinemas and multiplexes in mid-March 1993 were dominated by films in competition for Academy Awards in one category or another: *Scent of a Woman*, *Malcolm X*, *Lorenzo's Oil*, *A Few Good Men*, *A River Runs Through It* (all 1992). (*The Crying Game*, of course, was also a contender, eventually landing the Oscar for Best Original Screenplay.) *The Living End*, with its tiny budget, punk attitude, and confrontational style and content, had more in common with other North American independent films screening in the art cinemas that week: *Slacker* (1990) and *Reservoir Dogs* (1992). Then as now, I would happily sit through (almost) all of the movies being released, mainstream or otherwise, basking in the pleasures afforded by any trip to the cinema; my own tastes were solidifying, however, and the late 1980s and early 1990s boom in American independent cinema had a profound impact on my understandings of what film could be.

The Living End, at that first exposure, felt like a breath of fresh air. It was scuzzy and sexy, barrelled along at a serious clip, and wasn't afraid of jarring tonal shifts. Though I'm sure I missed some of the allusions to other films, *The Living End*'s evident love of the power of popular music and cinema, and its aesthetic delight in late twentieth century cultural detritus, provided palpable pleasures. Clearly, this was not another iteration of the sad lesbian and gay cinema that I had gulped down across my teenage years (whether *The Children's Hour* [1961] or *The Killing of Sister George* [1968]), which had a troubling impact on my understanding of my own queerness. Here, in contrast, was an alternative worldview. From start to finish, from Luke graffitiing the words "Fuck the World" in blood-red spray paint to the final credit lambasting "a big white house full of republican fuckheads," the film was evidently driven by a sense of fury at the ongoing HIV epidemic and the social and political marginalisation of queer people. Its anger rhymed with my own simmering activist rage.

In the early 1990s, for the first time I found myself part of a sizeable and highly sociable queer community – one that was varied and inclusive in terms of sexual orientation and gender expression, and which was intergenerational and racially and ethnically diverse. These were people with whom to party, bicker, have sex. Though I have now lost touch with almost all of them – at the end of my years as an undergraduate, many of us moved on to new cities and new lives – I owe a great deal to these people, who significantly influenced my tastes, my politics, and my sense of humour. Crucially, this group was undergirded by an activist politics that sometimes manifested in direct action. Thatcher may have been ousted in 1990, but we were still living under Tory rule, and the legacy of the Iron Lady persisted. Section 28 had been introduced into law in 1988: this was an article of Conservative Party legislation which outlawed local authorities from "promoting homosexuality"; schools could not recognise or endorse "the acceptability of homosexuality as a pretended family relationship." This legislation produced a culture of fear around openly discussing sexuality, especially in education. Although ultimately no local councils were prosecuted under Section 28, its very existence encouraged the marginalisation and persecution of queer people. As did the Tory government's messaging on HIV and AIDS: the expensive "Don't Die of Ignorance" public information campaign of 1987 included memorable adverts shown in cinemas and on television, which featured sinister footage of tombstones and icebergs. "So far it has been confined to small groups," John Hurt stated on the audio track of the "Monolith" advert, "but it's spreading." Heterosexual audiences were encouraged to see queers as infected, infectious, a source of dirt and threat. As an undergraduate student, I befriended a fair number of young men who were HIV positive, my own age or slightly older, many of whom swiftly succumbed to AIDS. Each loss was a distressing and painful shock.

After seeing *The Living End*, I developed an auteurist fascination with Araki's work. To this day, he is one of the very few directors all of whose films I have seen multiple times. When, in 1997, I submitted a proposal for a PhD on New Queer Cinema to a number of universities in the United Kingdom, Araki featured as a pivotal figure for analysis. (The tentative title for that thesis, which I quickly shed, was "Still Life Without Fruit"; there is a book still to be written with this title). As I began my academic career at the turn of the century, I was invited to write about Araki and his work, publishing two pieces on him in edited collections.[1] I was struggling to find my scholarly voice, and attempted to both capture the rebellious, ambivalent, often sardonic register of Araki's films and also emulate the style of writers I admired (journalists Paul Burston, Richard Smith, Sylvia Patterson, Lucy O'Brien; filmmaker Bruce LaBruce; my PhD supervisor Andy Medhurst, who disliked Araki's films but always supported my research and writing). I am now sorely embarrassed by these pieces, which I find opinionated and glib, marred by a lack of balance and generosity. My editors were incredibly supportive, and I remain indebted to them, though I knew at the time that both essays failed to respectfully fulfil the remit of the collections in which they appeared. Looking back, I wish I had been able to find a more appropriate way to articulate my esteem for Araki's work, its complexity and nuances, its textures and tenors, its pleasures and politics. I only hope this short book begins to provide that atonement.

Acknowledgments

First and foremost, an enormous and heartfelt thanks to the editors of the Queer Film Classics series, Tom Waugh and Matthew Hays: for their unwavering support for this volume, for their patience and leniency, for their gentle chivvies and generous feedback. I could not have written this book without a wealth of valuable resources that Gary Needham provided early on in the research process; Jacob Engelberg also helped me out with an especially hard-to-find source. Gary helpfully reviewed a full first draft and provided thoughtful insights which prompted some considerable alterations to the final manuscript. I am enormously grateful to all of the people with whom I have discussed Araki's films over the last thirty years, particularly Kay Dickinson, Jonathan Flatley, Greg Goldberg, Andy Medhurst, Mandy Merck, Monica Pearl, Marc Siegel, and Lizzie Thynne. Michele Aaron and Yvonne Tasker supported my early, flawed attempts to write about Araki and his films: I owe them both immeasurably. Last but not least, my thanks to the fantastic people at MQUP, especially Jonathan Crago, who (like all the best editors) managed to say the right things at exactly the right times.

Synopsis

Los Angeles, present day. Jon, a film journalist, receives the result of his first HIV test: he is seropositive. Driving around the city, he records his thoughts into a Dictaphone. Luke, a rootless drifter, is hitchhiking. Daisy and Fern, a psychotic lesbian couple in a coupe, pick him up. They threaten to murder him, but he manages to escape with their car and gun. When the vehicle gets a flat tire, he abandons it. Jon discloses his new HIV-positive status to his best friend, Darcy, an artist; he suspects the source of the infection was his ex, Craig. Back at his apartment, Jon broods and listens back to his Dictaphone journal entries.

Luke, hitching again, is picked up by Ken. Back at Ken's apartment, Luke spanks him with a tennis racket. Later, as the two doze in bed, Ken's wife Barbie returns home and, furious at finding him with another man, stabs him to death with a large kitchen knife. Luke flees. As he catches his breath in a parking lot, three homophobes with baseball bats accost him. Luke shoots all three dead.

Jon, driving around the city at night, is flagged down by Luke, running from the scene of the crime. Jon takes Luke back to his apartment, where the two reveal their shared HIV-positive status and have sex. Over breakfast the next morning, Luke voices his opinion that being HIV positive means they have "nothing to lose": "We can do anything we want." They go shopping using a credit card that Luke stole from Ken. Carrying their new purchases on the street, they bump into a neo-Nazi who verbally abuses them. Luke bludgeons the man with a boombox; he and Jon scarper. Exasperated by Luke's behaviour, Jon kicks Luke out of his apartment, but soon misses him.

Jon wakes to find Luke in his bedroom. Luke has the gun between his lips and his face is spattered with blood; he thinks he may have killed a cop. The two go on the run – first to San Francisco, where Luke thinks they can hide out with a friend, Gus. However, when they arrive in the city, Gus shuts the door in Luke's face. Jon and Luke take to the road, bantering and bickering, fucking, crashing in motels, and living on trashy fast food. Luke suggests that they drive to Washington and murder the President or inject him with their infected blood, but Jon dismisses his daydream. Intermittently, Jon phones Darcy to check in; she becomes increasingly concerned about him. Jon, running out of patience with Luke's impetuous behaviour, threatens to leave and go home. Luke talks him down, and the pair continue their travels. Darcy and her boyfriend Peter argue. Peter reveals he has started seeing someone else, and Darcy kicks him out.

In a conversation about death, Luke tells Jon that he wants Jon to kill him. Jon's health starts to suffer. Running low on money, the pair stop at an ATM, but it is out of order: Luke shoots it, setting off alarms. His tolerance exhausted, Jon decides to go home, and phones Darcy to tell her. When Luke cuts open his arm to inspect his blood, Jon hits him, announcing that their "hackneyed romantic fantasy" is over. Luke pulls the gun on Jon and knocks him out with it. When Jon comes around, he is tied up on a beach. Luke pulls off Jon's trousers and underwear and fucks him, with the gun in his own mouth. At the point of orgasm, he pulls the trigger, but the weapon has run out of bullets. Jon punches Luke and walks away – but he returns, and the two sit on the sand, intimate, as the sun drops over the ocean.

Credits

Cast in order of appearance:[1]

Luke: Mike Dytri
Jon: Craig Gilmore
Doctor: Mark Finch
Daisy: Mary Woronov
Fern: Johanna Went
Darcy: Darcy Marta
Peter: Scot Goetz
Ken: Bretton Vail
Barbie: Nicole Dillenberg
7-Eleven couple: Stephen Holman, Magie Song
Three stooges: Peter Lanigan, Jon Gerrans, Jack Kofman
Melrose neo-Nazi: Christopher Mabli
Tarzan: Michael Now
Jane: Michael Haynes
Gus: Peter Gramé
Ralphs couple: Craig Lee, Torie Chickering
Buddhist: J. Sidney Beswick

Written, directed, photographed, and edited by Gregg Araki
Producers: Marcus Hu, Jon Gerrans
Associate producer: Andrea Sperling

Co-producer: Jim Stark
Executive producers: Evelyn Hu, Jon Jost, Henry Rosenthal, Mike Thomas
Lighting: Christopher Münch
Sound recordists: Dave Cash, Joyce Brouwers, Jack Kofman
Assistant editor: Tommy Huie
Sound designer: George Lockwood
Assistant sound: Marianne Dissard
Post-production sound remixing: Muscle & Hate Studios
Original music composed by: Cole Coonce
Benevolent music gods: Matt Adell and Jim Nash at Wax Trax! Records
Titles shot by: Mar Elepano
Title design: Steven Hankinson
Negative cutting: Karen Kennedy
Stills: Michael Matson
Graphic design: Steven Hankinson
Props: Johanna Went
Paintings by: Beth Muehl

Song credits:

"Where the Pavement Ends," written by C. Coonce/W. Croyle, performed by Braindead Sound Machine, published by Braindead Muzick.

"Reactionary Lezbos with Gun Theme," written by C. Coonce/R. Weeks, performed by Cambodia, published by Braindead Muzick.

"Synaesthesia," "Cords of Love," written by Chris Carter/Cosey Fanni Tutti, performed by Chris and Cosey, published by S.C. Confidence.

"The Snow," "Further Back and Faster," written by Coil, performed by Coil, published by Threshold House.

"Rosebud," "Suburbarenity," written by Fred Giannelli, performed by Fred, published by Turning Shrines Unlimited.

"I Wanna Go to Hell," "Godlike," "Naïve," written by KMFDM, performed by KMFDM, published by Freibank/Les Editions Confidentielles.

"Jigsaw," "I.C. Water," written by F. Giannelli/G. P-Orridge, performed by Psychic TV, published by Complete Music.
The above appear courtesy of Wax Trax! Records.

"Mask," "Smrow-toh," "Reality," "Mindfuck," written and performed by Babyland, published by/courtesy of F.S. Records.
"Agress," "Decisions," "Ingest," written and performed by Biohazard PCB, published by/courtesy of PCB Productions.
"Filament," "Blunt Force Trauma," written and performed by Chem Lab, published by/courtesy of Fifth Column Records.
"Countdown," "Caliber," written and performed by Drance, published by Justa Thang, courtesy of Slamjam/Dr Dream Records.
"Hate River," "Imitation," "Hang Your Head," written and performed by 16Volt, published by E. Powell/Ink Head Productions.

Desperate thanks to:

Bob Beverly, Cinema Products, John Cooper, Stuart Cornfeld, Morgan Fisher, Rose Guzman, Hart Video, Natalie Hashimoto, Ray Holmes, Nietzchka Keene, Claudia Lewis, Ian Love, Jim Mack, Tammye McDavid, Omelette Parlor, Phil, Bill and Elaine at PBRS, Paul Rutan, Rosebud Café, Charlie Schlissel, Joseph Shak, Mr Shipman, Sundance Institute, Travel Lodge Motels, Chris Walas Inc., Angela Yee, My Mom and Dad.

This film received a production grant from the American Film Institute, in association with the National Endowment for the Arts.

Dedicated to Craig Lee (1954–1991) and the hundreds of thousands who've died and the hundreds of thousands more who will die because of a big white house full of republican fuckheads.

THE LIVING END

Introduction
Fuck the World

Gregg Araki was born in December 1959 and raised on the West Coast of the United States, north of Los Angeles. A third generation Japanese American, he grew up in Santa Barbara, in an environment he describes as "very white, very middle class suburbia" (Chua 1992, 27–8). He gained a BA in film studies in 1982 from UC Santa Barbara, where the critical perspective taught was traditionally auteurist: John Ford, Jean Renoir, Fritz Lang, all seen through the lens of such authors as Andrew Sarris. A submersion in Jean-Luc Godard's cinema through a course taught by Michael Renov was especially influential. As Araki would later tell Chris Chang, "The films from *Breathless* [*À bout de souffle*, 1960] to *Week-end* [1967] were totally formative and became part of my experience. I like some of the later films and I don't like some of the others, but the output from '59 to '69 is just phenomenal" (Chang 1994, 53). Araki went on to study for an MFA at the University of Southern California where, as B. Ruby Rich writes, "he was supposed to learn industry standards and three-act structures but instead proved himself 'a pretentious dickhead' who kept bringing up Godard" (Rich 2013, 94). He graduated from USC in 1985.

In the second half of the 1980s Araki made two micro-budget feature films, *Three Bewildered People in the Night* (1987) and *The Long Weekend (O' Despair)* (1989), for around $5,000 each. He shot them on a Bolex in 16 mm using Kodak Tri-X, a versatile and high-contrast black-and-white stock which is able to register images in low light, and made them without sync sound, recording and adding audio later. *Three Bewildered People* focuses on the lives of Alicia (Darcy Marta), a video artist; her boyfriend Craig (John Lacques), an actor and photographer between jobs; and her gay best friend David (Mark Howell), a performance artist. Alicia and David struggle to make work. Conversations between the three characters, mainly configured in pairs, unfurl over coffee and cigarettes in an array of Los Angeles locations: diners, galleries, parking lots, cluttered apartments. David sports an eye patch, perhaps a nod to the lineage of auteur film directors who also wore one (Nicholas Ray, John Ford, Fritz Lang). Attraction simmers between Craig and David but remains unconsummated. The film's erotic triad configuration (two men, one woman, suggestions of or overt engagement with heteroflexibility and bisexuality) is one to which Araki would return in the 1990s, with *The Doom Generation* (1995) and *Splendor* (1999). *Variety* disliked *Three Bewildered People*, saying the film had "little to recommend it" ("Edna" 1987). In contrast, in the programme for the Twelfth San Francisco International Gay and Lesbian Film Festival, held in June 1988, Paul Bollwinkel described the film as "refreshing [and] often wryly funny," praising Araki for "a remarkable job with a limited budget" (Bollwinkel 1988). *Three Bewildered People* was one of three films awarded the Bronze Leopard at the Locarno Film Festival in 1987.

In *The Long Weekend*, Araki increased the size of his cast, if not of his budget. The plot concerns a group of friends who gather for a college reunion, only to discover their feelings of nostalgia may have been misplaced. The film's three couples – two men, two women, and one of each – find their relationships tested by the experience. British writer and film programmer Mark Finch wittily praised the film:

> It's *twentysomething* set by the light of a shopping mall, where all the characters are too doped up or simply can't stop talking … *The Long Weekend* is what gay cinema ought to be – droll, detached and undetermined. [It] also chaperones this year's Major Theme in Gay Male movies: bisexual melancholy. This is about modern youngsters who can't decide whether they crave relationships with the same sex, the opposite sex, or with their complete collection of The Smiths singles. (Finch 1989)

Though still expressing major reservations, *Variety* was more enamoured of Araki's second film than his first, praising the director for managing "to convey a sporadically amusing world view on the most limited of means." For the reviewer, Araki "comes to embody the antithesis of the traditional well-made, slick industry 'product,' which makes him a needed banner carrier for a certain fringe of the independent movement" ("Cart" 1989). At the Los Angeles Film Critics Association Awards for 1989, *The Long Weekend* won the Experimental/Independent Film/Video Award.

Chris Chang and Daryl Chin both provide valuable analyses of *Three Bewildered People* and *The Long Weekend*. Chang identifies these films as "entropic studies in disintegrating relationships" which take place in a "practically motionless world nonetheless saturated with psychic pain." For him, Araki's use of the Bolex hampered what could be achieved: "One feels the limitations of the technology straining against the poetics. In some cases an empty frame is established that you wish you could linger over, examine closer, fall into." Chang suggests that the post-sync sound, however, heightens the impact of both films: "The dub adds a hollowness to the sound, a displaced quality that enhances the pervasive helplessness, an amputation of frequency response that adds sonically challenged to the checklist of character disabilities" (Chang 1994, 50). For Chin, both films are "not easy to watch." Araki's narratives, he writes, "do not flow. Rather, they proceed through ellipses, blockages, emptiness, devices which break the continuity to allow for breathing." He praises the director's visual aesthetic, especially his "compositional boldness" and his ability to capture "the quality of light within the artificially lit urban landscape." In these black-and-white films, "Araki's images often have the quality of charcoal smudges, with the film's graininess causing shades of grey and black to bleed together" (Chin 1993, 106). I will return to Chin's comments on form and aesthetics in chapter 3 when unpacking these dimensions of *The Living End*.

Although *Three Bewildered People* and *The Long Weekend* are certainly "entropic studies," intimate character studies that foster a sense of claustrophobia, the latter engages with a broader cultural and political context, however partially. The film studies syllabus makes a brief appearance: Michael (Bretton Vail) flips through one of the two volumes of André Bazin's *What Is Cinema?*, then drops both in the trash. (Bazin resurfaces in Araki's *Totally F***ed Up* [1994], similarly dismissively: a character leans on a book by the critic to take down a phone number.) More significantly, HIV/AIDS affects the lives of the characters in *The Long Weekend*. Print media coverage is acknowledged: early in the film, as Michael cleans his apartment, we see a copy of LA *Weekly* with the headline "AIDS" on the cover (figure 1). Later, as the same character watches television with his friend Sara (Nicole Dillenberg), we see an advert for a fearmongering book titled *Crisis: Heterosexual Behaviour in the Age of* AIDS. A pull quote from the book appears over an image of its cover, highlighting the circulation of false and menacing information: "It is theoretically possible to become infected with the AIDS virus from skin contact with a contaminated toilet seat" (figure 2). Characters discuss the negative consequences of sex, including potential infection, with one saying, "you're fucked whatever one's choice of genital alignment." These elements serve as a glancing preview of the more sustained engagement with HIV/AIDS that *The Living End* offers.

The first screenplay for *The Living End* was written in 1988, while Araki was editing *The Long Weekend*. Originally titled *Fuck the World*, Araki says that the script "came from a very dark, personal place – those feelings of dread and insecurity which characterized the mid-late '80s AIDS crisis pervaded the consciousness of my whole generation." He asked himself probing questions: "What *would* I do if I tested positive? How would I feel? What would my reaction be?" The first draft of the script ended with both Jon and Luke dead; as Araki says, "I thought 'Wow, this is too depressing for even *me* to produce'" (Araki 1992). He parked the screenplay and began to work on what would become his fourth feature film, *Totally F***ed Up*. While developing that project,

Figures 1 and 2
Mediated references to AIDS in *The Long Weekend (O' Despair)* (1989).

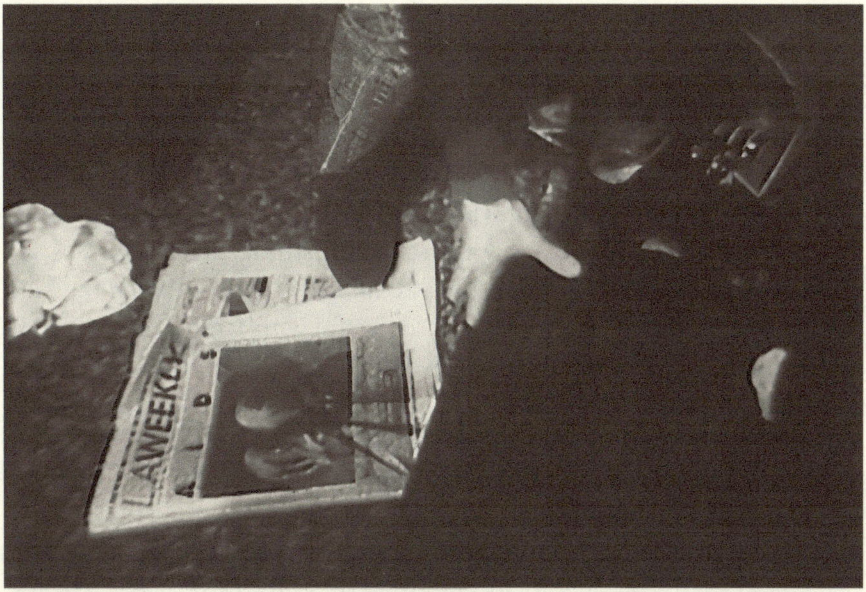
LAWEEKLY

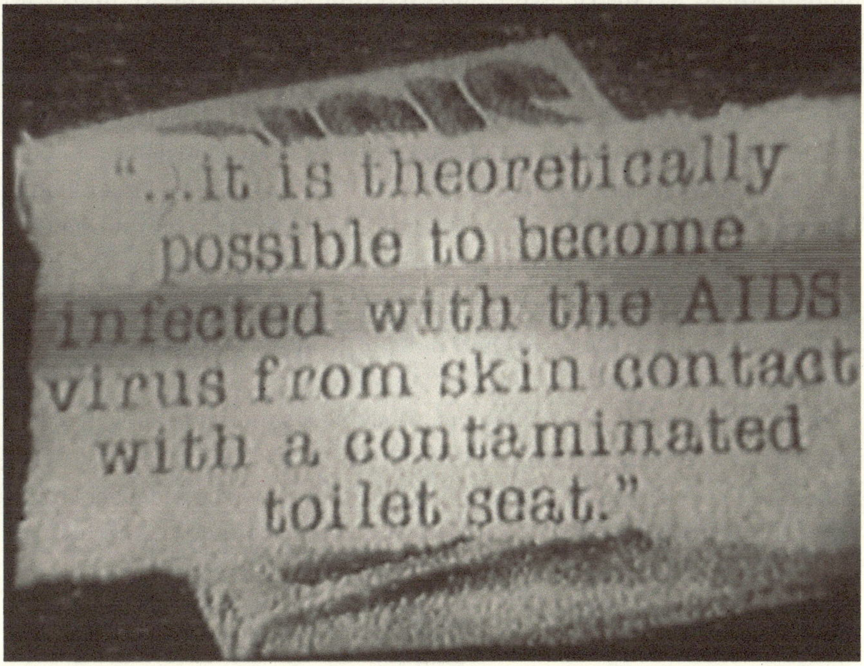
"...it is theoretically
possible to become
infected with the AIDS
virus from skin contact
with a contaminated
toilet seat."

Araki met Marcus Hu through the gay film festival circuit. Hu voiced an interest in financing one of Araki's movies, which prompted Araki to rewrite the script of *The Living End.*

Hu – along with Mike Thomas and Jon Gerrans – co-founded Strand Releasing, a distribution company that is still going strong. In the late 1980s, Hu was a programmer at the Strand Theatre in San Francisco. When the Lino Brocka film *Macho Dancer* (1988) was successful with Strand audiences, Hu and Thomas (the Strand's manager) worked with Brocka to independently distribute it in the United States. This led Hu, Thomas, and Gerrans to form Strand Releasing in 1989. *The Living End* was the first time that the company had tried its hand at production, rather than distribution. (Gerrans, incidentally, has a cameo in the film as one of the three homophobes Luke shoots.) Over the decades, Strand has handled a variety of titles, including a substantial slate of auteur-driven global arthouse cinema. As Bryan Wuest writes, "Although Strand has distributed – and even produced – plenty of films with LGBT content and has many cultural associations with LGBT film, the company has always had an ambivalent relationship to the actual category of 'LGBT'" (Wuest 2018, 37). Hu claims in a 1994 interview that "we look for quality films, and just because it's gay doesn't mean we're going to handle it. It has to be a good movie before we'll take care of it" (Lally 1994, 10). The company's involvement with the New Queer Cinema film movement was substantial, however. "Strand's founding was key to the initial flowering of the NQC [New Queer Cinema]," writes Rich; years later, their "dedication to bringing back many of the films of the early 1990s in high-quality DVD formats [was] key to preserving NQC history" (Rich 2013, 32).

Araki conceived of *The Living End* as having a similar no-budget, black-and-white style to his first two features. However, speaking on a panel at the Sundance Producers' Conference in 1990, he met maverick independent director Jon Jost, whose *All the Vermeers in New York* (1990) was garnering critical attention and praise. As Araki says, "I guess [he] felt sympathetic towards me as he generously offered the use of his sync-sound camera equipment as well as some leftover Fuji film stock" (Araki 1992). Araki purchased some Kodak 7296 stock to supplement Jost's gift, which meant that the film could be shot in colour with sync sound. *The Living End* was still a micro-budget shoot, costing just $22,769 to make.[1] Production was able to begin with a financial loan from a relative, with further piecemeal donations raised along the way. "We never really had a budget, we just started to shoot," says Araki. "I felt very confident because I'd made two films before. I always knew the film would get done" (Broderick 1992/1993). The production adopted guerrilla methods: filming without permits, calling in favours, and using a minimal cast and crew, none of whom were paid. *The Living End* screenplay was very tightly written: "All of my films are scripted out to every uh, uh-huh, dot dot dot, and yeah," Araki tells Chris Chang. "Every little thing is in there. It's so much more economical because you can't make one of those improvisatory movies without a 50-to-1 shooting ratio" (Chang 1994, 50). Araki also previsualises all of his films: as he told Matthew Hays in 2006, "To this day, I draw simple storyboards of every shot and scene in my films. They serve as comic-book-like visualisations of my movies. I've always worked in this way since I made my first student films in college" (Hays 2007, 37).

The Living End was shot sporadically in autumn and winter of 1990, working around actors' schedules and Araki's promotional duties for *The Long Weekend*. "We tended not to shoot really full days," Araki says. "We usually shot no more than eight hours, and often less. I don't believe in the army mentality of everybody up at 6:30 and march till sunrise" (Broderick 1992/1993). According to Mike Dytri, who played Luke, the shoot was interrupted for several weeks after he sustained a facial injury and needed stitches. To avoid the crew having to travel too far, Hu sent some film stock to Richard Linklater and asked him to record some "road movie" footage in Texas, which he dutifully did, although his contribution went uncredited. Araki's final shooting ratio was in the region of five-to-one. As filming came to an end, the American Film Institute provided the director with a production grant of $20,000, which covered around 85 per cent of the budget.

Araki edited *The Living End* on a Moviola in his apartment, but the process stalled when funding was secured for *Totally F***ed Up*. He shot his fourth feature in spring and summer of 1991, and then returned to editing *The Living End*, completing a cut in November 1991. The two films are intertwined in many ways: from slogans (Luke scrawls "I Blame Society" on a parking lot pillar, figure 3; Andy [James Duval] wears a T-shirt featuring the same words in *Totally F***ed Up*, figure 4) to actors (Craig Gilmore and Johanna Went have cameos in the later film). Post-production on *The Living End* (sound editing and mixing, negative cutting, and so on) was done over the holiday period. The film screened at the Sundance Film Festival in January 1992, where it was nominated for a Grand Jury Prize (award winners that year included Christopher Münch's *The Hours and Times* [1991] and Tom Kalin's *Swoon* [1992]). The film's co-producer, Jim Stark, had promotional badges made that read, "When I start to come, choke me" (a ribald line from the film), which were widely distributed at the event. Sundance in 1992 was one of the festivals at which New Queer Cinema took shape and broke through: B. Ruby Rich chaired a discussion panel on the topic of queer film entitled "Barbed Wire Kisses," whose contributors included Derek Jarman, Isaac Julien, Todd Haynes, Tom Kalin, and Sadie Benning – but not Araki, though he was in the audience. Robert Redford, a figurehead of the festival, gave a press conference at which he was asked why there were so many gay films in the programme. According to Rich, Redford responded that these works were "all part of the spectrum of independent film that Sundance is meant to serve" (Rich 1992, 32).

Independent producer and writer John Pierson saw *The Living End* at Sundance, judging it "effective, energetic, promotable, and, ultimately, likely to

Figures 3 and 4
The slogan "I Blame Society" serves as one link between *The Living End* (1992) and *Totally F***ed Up* (1994).

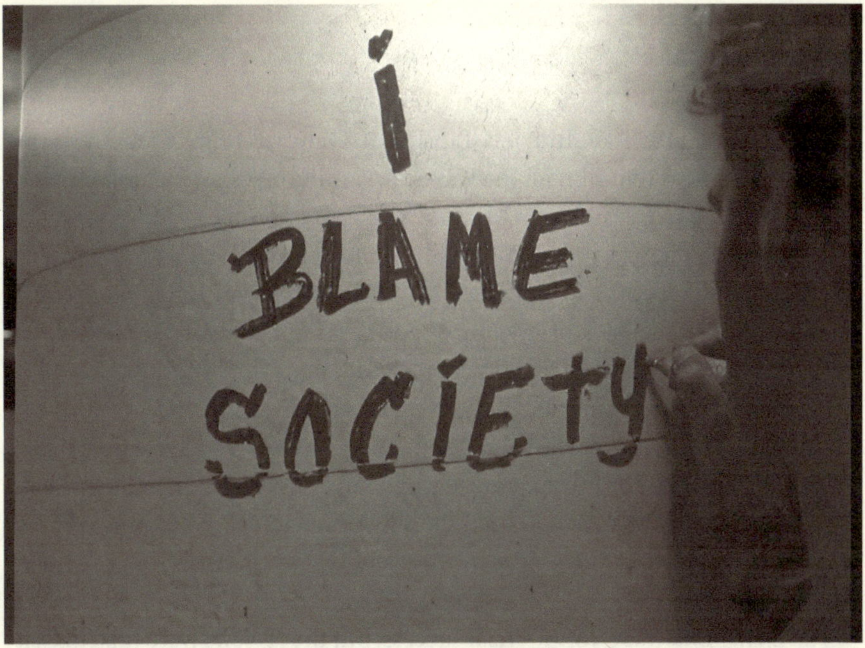
I BLAME SOCIETY

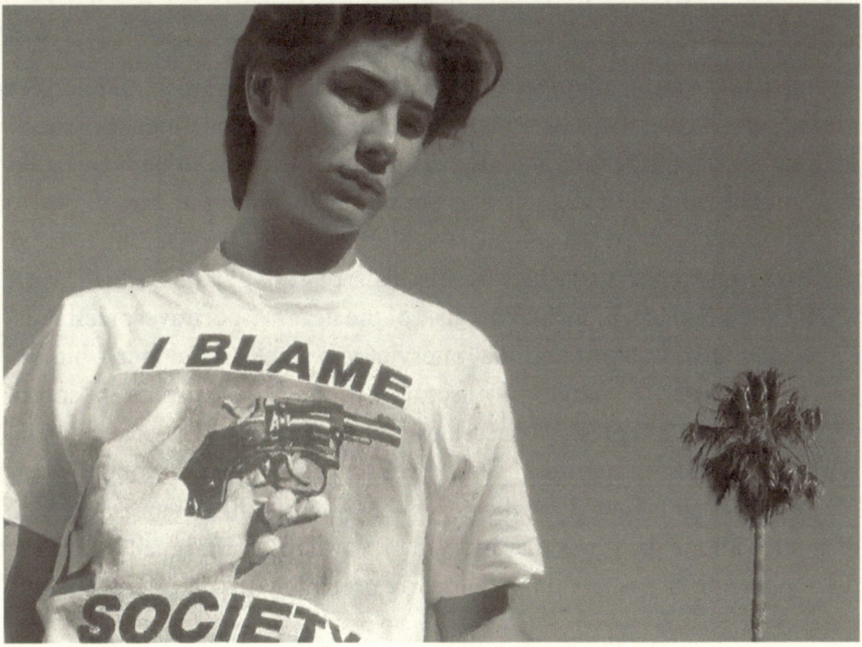
I BLAME
SOCIET

succeed." Bingham Ray and Jeff Lipsky of October Films "felt the same way. They worked that film all the way to a $1 million gross, making it one of the Sundance success stories" (Pierson 1996, 210). October spent money on improving the picture and sound quality, and on making a 35 mm blowup. *The Living End* was officially released into cinemas in the United States on 21 August 1992. "In the back of my mind," Araki says, "I was sort of hoping that by the time *The Living End* was finally released, the AIDS holocaust would be over and the movie would be something of an anachronism" (Araki 1992). Craig Gilmore remembers the film's popularity: "When it was released, in San Francisco, it played for I think ten days of sold-out performances, 1400 seats. The Angelika in New York had lines literally up the block. Madonna came to see it … For two weeks it was the most-attended film in America per screen" ("Pioneers" 2022).

The Living End was a commercial success, but the reviews were mixed. Critics repeatedly voiced concerns about the film's representations of women and lesbians. Steve Warren, in the *San Francisco Sentinel*, queried Araki's use of stereotypes – "I guess icepick-wielding dykes are acceptable in queer movies" – while Trudy Ring, in *Outlines*, criticised both the lesbian killers and Barbie's murder of Ken: "Perhaps Araki intends these scenes to be tongue-in-cheek, sending up the misogynist stereotypes that hold lesbians to be man-haters and straight women to be fools – or perhaps he believes the stereotypes. At any rate, these scenes don't enhance the film" (Warren 1992, 30; Ring 1992, 28, 40). Araki remembers that "there were lesbians picketing at the Castro Theatre when it played in San Francisco because of the negative portrayal of lesbians" ("Pioneers" 2022). In promotional interviews for the film, he found himself having to answer to charges of misogyny. Talking to Mansel Stimpson of *Capital Gay*, Araki expressed concern over the accusations: "In fact, feminism is a big influence on me, and I very much respect women. Throughout my life my best friends have always been women. And I think that the oppression of women and of gays goes very much hand-in-hand." He argued that "all of the supporting characters" in the film "are presented in a garish, almost cartoonish, satirical way," and that the secondary women characters should not be seen as representative of what "Gregg Araki thinks of women" (Stimpson 1993). Lizzie Francke, reviewing the film in *Sight and Sound*, recognised this distinction: "The depiction of women is open to criticism," she wrote, but beyond the film's core characters the rest are "pop-up ciphers who are negligible in the final analysis" (Francke 1993, 50).

A number of reviewers found much to acclaim in Araki's film. Francke praised *The Living End* for "an energy that belies its impoverished finances," drawing attention to its "Californian sun-scalded images." "Aesthetically and politically," she wrote, "this is an instant film"; however, she described the ending as "dangerously lacking in hope" (Francke 1993, 50). Warren concluded, more positively, that "*The Living End* will make you feel angry, horny and in a perverse way, happy. It's often quite funny, in a very dark way. Queer cinema is designed to provoke as well as entertain, and this is as queer as they come" (Warren 1992, 30). Steve Davis, in the *Austin Chronicle*, called it "a road movie that leaves a skid mark on the psyche," arguing that "Araki taps into something very primal in the film's depiction of its two opposites that attract" (Steve Davis 1992). And Janet Maslin in *The New York Times* was effulgent in her praise, writing that the film "has the power of honesty and originality, as well as the weight of legitimate frustration. Miraculously, it also has a buoyant, mischievous spirit that transcends any hint of gloom" (Maslin 1992).

In this book, I provide a sustained analysis of *The Living End* – its production context, the live and thorny political topics with which it engages, its form and content. In chapter 1, I explore Araki's film as a pivotal contribution to what B. Ruby Rich named "New Queer Cinema," a short-lived efflorescence of independent queer film and video that made a mark at festivals and generated a sturdy volume of critical discussion in the early 1990s. I unpack the queer moment of the late 1980s and early 1990s, and how decisive shifts away from earlier lesbian and gay politics, activism, and forms of representation were attempted. I pay attention to the "positive images" debate and how New Queer Cinema intervened in the conversation. Further, I explore the status and significance of *The Living End* as an independent film. In chapter 2, I engage at length with perhaps the most important context in which New Queer Cinema situated itself, and with which it engaged: the HIV/AIDS pandemic, then at its height. I examine the politics of HIV/AIDS representation, queer film and video responses to the pandemic, and the ways in which New Queer Cinema, in particular, offered alternative strategies for depicting and raising awareness of HIV/AIDS. In chapter 3, I dig into the content of *The Living End*, exploring its generic form, its uses of pastiche, appropriation and intertextuality, its mise-en-scène, and its soundtrack. Finally, in a brief coda, I reflect on the film's legacy and on Araki's subsequent career.

Chapter 1
New Queer Cinema, Revisited

In 1992, having attended a number of recent film festivals screening a significant volume of independent lesbian and gay work, cultural critic B. Ruby Rich wrote an article for the *Village Voice*. In "A Queer Sensation," which appeared in the 24 March 1992 issue, she suggests that many of these films shared particular qualities. Later that year, in September, British magazine *Sight and Sound* reprinted the essay with the headline "New Queer Cinema." The reprint was supplemented by a number of shorter articles responding to Rich's essay, fleshing out context, and commenting on some of the films she discusses. Rich later remembered that the New Queer Cinema moniker "originated in a conversation I had with Philip Dodd, then the editor in chief [of *Sight and Sound*], about how I viewed developments since the *Voice* piece had been published. It is to that conversation that I owe the serendipity of my term's immortalization as a title and, later, movement" (Rich 2013, 31). To coincide with the publication of Rich's essay in *Sight and Sound*, London's Institute of Contemporary Arts organised a three-day international conference on New Queer Cinema.

At Toronto's Festival of Festivals (now Toronto International Film Festival) in September 1991, Rich had first noticed "a flock of films that were doing something new, renegotiating subjectivities, annexing whole genres, revising histories in their image" (Rich 1992, 31). These included short films (Laurie

Lynd's RSVP, Su Friedrich's *First Comes Love*, John Greyson's *The Making of "Monsters"*) and features (Gus Van Sant's *My Own Private Idaho*, Derek Jarman's *Edward II*). Two months later at Amsterdam's Gay and Lesbian Film Festival, she noted "a contemporary lesbian sensibility" surfacing in several videos (Rich 1992, 33). Key examples included Cecilia Dougherty's *Grapefruit* (1989), Cecilia Barriga's *The Meeting of Two Queens* (1991), and Kaucyila Brooke and Jane Cottis's *Dry Kisses Only* (1990). The Sundance Film Festival of January 1992 served as a vital showcase for the new cluster of queer work: here, Rich argues, the "sense of a historical moment ... now burst into full view" (Rich 2013, 27). *Edward II* and RSVP were screened, as were *The Living End*, *Swoon*, *The Hours and Times*, and *Young Soul Rebels* – all directed by men. Rich's "Barbed Wire Kisses" panel at that festival began with a screening of Sadie Benning's *Jollies*, intended to draw attention to gendered inequalities and barriers to access ingrained in the film industry. Indeed, Rich clearly articulates her dismay about the gender division evident with the new queer work: "Surprise, all the new movies being snatched up by distributors, shown in mainstream festivals, booked into theatres, are by the boys. Surprise, the amazing new lesbian videos that are redefining the whole dyke relationship to popular culture remain hard to find" (Rich 1992, 32). Not that this prevents Rich from praising key works by "the boys." In her overview of the Sundance showings, she notes of *The Living End* that "early Araki films are often too garage-band, too boychick, too far into visual noise, but this one is different." Rich judges the film as one that "deserves a place in movie history – an existential film for a post-porn age, one that puts queers on the map as legitimate genre subjects" (Rich 1992, 34).

In her "New Queer Cinema" article, Rich attempts a summation of what bound these films of the moment together, whilst recognising the challenges of doing so:

> Of course, the new queer films and videos aren't all the same and don't share a single aesthetic vocabulary, strategy, or concern. Yet they are

> nonetheless united by a common style. Call it "Homo Pomo": there are traces in all of them of appropriation and pastiche, irony, as well as a reworking of history with social constructionism very much in mind. Definitively breaking with older humanist approaches and the films and tapes that accompanied identity politics, these works are irreverent, energetic, alternately minimalist and excessive. Above all, they're full of pleasure. (Rich 1992, 32)

These tantalising lines have become the standard reference quote in any critical or theoretical engagement with New Queer Cinema. I will discuss the style of *The Living End* – including its uses of appropriation and pastiche, as well as its minimalism and excess – in substantive detail in chapter 3. Postmodernism, less so: "Homo Pomo" was a witty and catchy tag, but a problematic one. Since the 1990s postmodernism has lost a great deal of its critical currency as a concept and tool, in part due to the hubris of attempting a monolithic or overarching characterisation of the dominant aesthetics of an era, and in part because of its lack of political depth. As Michele Aaron writes, "In its apolitical foundations postmodernism provides a relevant but often distracting context for the discussion of NQC" (Aaron 2004, 5).

Some of the films Rich names or discusses in her 1992 essay fit well with her brisk characterisation of Homo Pomo. Take Todd Haynes's film *Poison* (1991), for instance, which won the Grand Jury Prize: Dramatic at Sundance in 1991. *Poison* is constructed from three interleaved narratives, each shot in a distinct manner: "Hero," a fake documentary about a young boy who murdered his father and, seemingly, flew away; "Horror," a black-and-white horror/science-fiction pastiche, centring on a scientist who imbibes a "sex serum" and transforms into an infectious monstrosity (figure 5); and "Homo," a prison-set tale of love between two inmates, reuniting after meeting as adolescents in a juvenile facility. Homage and appropriation are pivotal to the film's textures and effect, with Jean Genet's writings a dominant influence: "Homo," for example, lifts its setting, as well as some images and lines of dialogue, from *Miracle of the Rose* (1946). *Poison* foregrounds social constructionist understandings of identity: its protagonists are repeatedly labelled, framed, and thus "explained" by meaning-making bodies and representatives of dominant social forces (parents, teachers, the press, the legal system). The film's structure also offers an alternative to conventional narrative form. As Haynes states in an interview: "Heterosexuality to me is a structure as much as it is a content ... It's more exciting to think of revising, rethinking the ways that films are put together" (Wyatt 1993, 8). Further, across its varied elements, *Poison* plays with an array of tones, from knowingly camp (the excesses of "Horror") to unsettlingly oneiric (the stylised, theatrical pastoral scenes in "Homo").

In contrast, other films Rich mentions are less evidently Homo Pomo. Lynd's twenty-minute short *RSVP*, for example, focuses on Sid (Daniel MacIvor), who has recently lost his lover Andrew to AIDS. Listening to the CBC classical music request programme *RSVP* on the radio in his Toronto home, Sid realises that Andrew, in a letter submitted to the show prior to his death, asked to hear Jessye Norman's rendition of "Le spectre de la rose" from Berlioz's *Les Nuits d'Été* (figure 6). Due to Canada's staggered time zones and their associated broadcast lags, Sid is able to contact Andrew's sister Ellen in Winnipeg – and through her, Andrew's parents in the same city – to inform them about the programme and the request. They subsequently listen in. Norman's aria unites the main characters in their isolated grief, but also in one sequence touches a wider community of others all listening to the broadcast, including someone browsing in a bookstore, a worker in a queer community centre who pins Andrew's obituary to a noticeboard, and a waitress in a diner. The film ends with Andrew's father leaving a message on Sid's answerphone in which he thanks him for letting them know about the broadcast and acknowledges the role that Sid played in his son's life. *RSVP* is shot in a standard continuity style with naturalistic acting and only minor dialogue. Appropriation, pastiche, irony, and irreverence are notably absent. Rather, Lynd's film – which Thomas Waugh appositely describes as "crystalline" – is a poignant

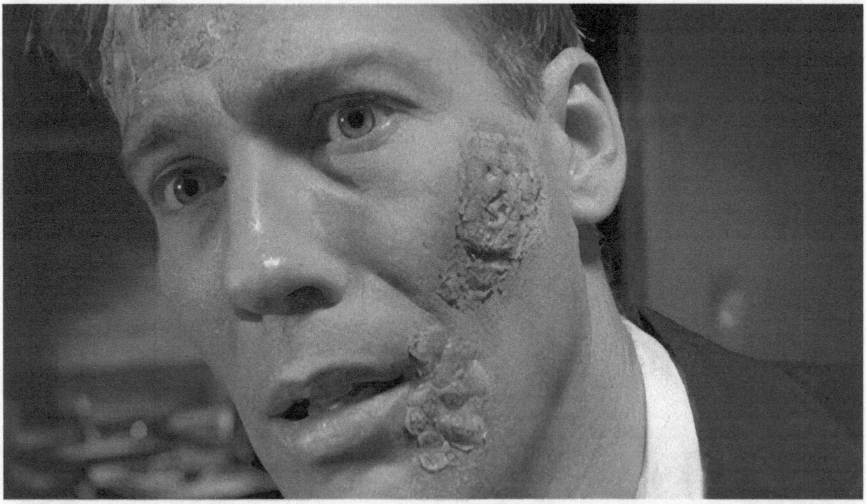

Figure 5
The "Horror" strand of Todd Haynes's film *Poison* pastiches horror and science-fiction films, focusing on the infection and monstrous transformation of Dr Graves (Larry Maxwell).

elegy for those lost to AIDS and conveys its resonant, layered narrative through simple and unshowy means (Waugh 2006, 280). Rich's argument that "Homo Pomo" is the glue that binds the movement's films, then, is open to question. Paul Burston raises this particular objection in *Time Out* magazine: David Lynch's films, he writes, are also "irreverent," "energetic," and "full of pleasure," "and I've yet to hear anyone claiming him as queer" (Burston 1995, 138).

Following her foundational 1992 essay, Rich has returned to the topic of New Queer Cinema on numerous occasions in her writing, elaborating and revising. Across the remainder of the 1990s, "queer cinema" swiftly became a niche market, facilitated by a roster of festivals and distribution companies. Major studios, through newly inaugurated boutique and arthouse divisions, started to support queer directors and their films. A more diverse array of

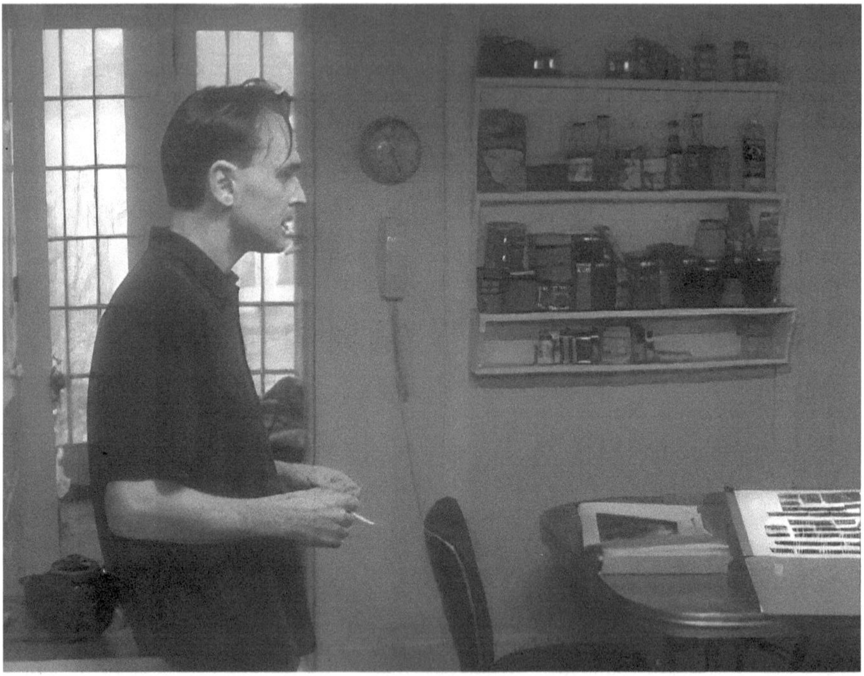

Figure 6
Sid (Daniel MacIvor) listens to Jessye Norman on the radio in Laurie Lynd's short film *RSVP* (1991).

queer characters and topics began to feature in mainstream cinema, with major stars signing on to play gay in films from *Philadelphia* (1993) to *The Talented Mr Ripley* (1999). A glut of queer-targeted work appeared, much of it mediocre. Reflecting on the decade in 2000, Rich writes that New Queer Cinema now looked more like "a moment than a movement," suggesting that it "had become so successful as to have dispersed itself in any number of elsewheres," transforming into "just another niche market, another product line pitched at one particular type of discerning consumer" (Rich 2000, 22, 24). Of course, the "moment" or "movement" was always a fabrication, a handy umbrella moniker for distributors and promoters to deploy as a marketing tool. As Gregg Araki puts it in interview, "When people ask me about the

Queer New Wave, I usually just half-jokingly say, 'Ask B. [Ruby Rich] about it,' because she invented it" (Smith 2008).

From the outset, individuals levelled criticisms at Rich's conception of the new wave of queer cinema. The essays that accompanied the *Sight and Sound* reprint of her essay contained challenges. For Derek Jarman, the widespread distribution of independent queer film might be a fresh experience in the United States, but it wasn't in the United Kingdom: his film *Sebastiane* (1976) had been shown in local cinemas across Britain (Jarman 1992). Pratibha Parmar describes New Queer Cinema as "a marketable, collective commodity produced by white gay men in the US," criticising queer film's lack of racial diversity. She also draws attention to other gaps in Rich's essay, highlighting "the obvious absence of a whole litany of lesbian filmmakers who aren't referenced" (Parmar 1992). In subsequent writings, others voice reservations and dissent. For Canadian filmmaker Bruce LaBruce, the New Queer Cinema label is "meaningless": "You see, I don't feel I have a lot in common with a bunch of rich kids with degrees in semiotic theory who make dry, academic films with overdetermined AIDS metaphors and Advocate Men in them" (LaBruce 1995, 194). (LaBruce's films are a striking omission in Rich's writings on New Queer Cinema: his witty and smutty *No Skin off My Ass* [1991], for one, arguably squares neatly with Rich's "Homo Pomo" formulation). Waugh is also sceptical, calling New Queer Cinema "an amnesiac semantic construction of the music video generation, because the queer cinema had been in a process of flux and accelerando since the late seventies and was anything but New" (Waugh 2000, 11).

Michele Aaron summarizes key concerns with Rich's thesis, calling New Queer Cinema "a contested category":

> It is contested for its exclusivity (and tokenistic inclusivity). It is contested for its unwarranted optimism: in heralding a minor revolution when a few films do not a movement make; in promoting queer villainy while homophobic violence rages; and in suggesting a queer-friendliness

> of mass culture when the vast majority of the audience ... remain unaltered. The category is also contested for the US-centricity of its films and theory. Perhaps the most irreparable of charges against NQC is that the promise indicated by the films of the early 1990s was never fully realised. (Aaron 2004, 8)

Despite these concerns, however, she sees the grouping together and critical interrogation of these films as a productive opportunity, "provoking and intervening within important discussions on the evolution of lesbian and gay representation, but also on the nature of cinema and spectatorship itself" (Aaron 2004, 11). Certainly, it is not my intention in this book to reify New Queer Cinema as a distinct, self-contained body of films bound together by a unifying aesthetic or political programme. Some of the titles associated with the "moment" share clear connections with others, but all require situating within more expansive histories of film production, including (as just one key strand) queer film history. Rich's formulation of New Queer Cinema is riddled with elisions and omissions. The moniker is perhaps most valuable as a temporal marker, a slippery referent that registers a globally productive period for queer moving-image work made outside of mainstream channels. Despite this, in the remainder of this chapter, I dig deeply into particular elements of Rich's original conceptualisation of New Queer Cinema and explore the ways in which they can provide a useful framing for *The Living End* and a deeper understanding of its significance. Specifically, I unpack the "queerness" of New Queer Cinema, the movement's (or moment's) relationship to the "positive images" debate, and its "independent" status.

The Queerness of New Queer Cinema

Rich's identification of New Queer Cinema in the early 1990s coincided with a politically motivated reclamation of the word "queer," with the appearance of a number of queer activist organisations, and with the genesis of queer theory. These shifts all took place internationally; here, I primarily focus on the context of the United States as the location within which Araki was making films. These developments had a substantive impact on how communities of queer people (and others) defined themselves, on the political priorities and attitudes expressed and articulated in activist practices and actions, and on the ways scholars from a broad array of disciplines approached and interpreted dissident sexualities and their wider implications.

Although the reader of a book in a series entitled "Queer Film Classics" is likely to know much of this history, it is worth reiterating in order to sketch out some of the contours of the cultural, political, and theoretical landscape into which *The Living End* landed and to which it contributed. Prior to the late 1980s, the word "queer" was almost always used as a term of abuse against sexual outlaws. The reclamation of the epithet attempted, as Richard Dyer notes, "not so much to cleanse it of its negative associations as to challenge the assumption that those associations are in fact negative – thus immorality may be a challenge to repressive morality, deviance a rejection of the straight and thus narrow, and what is considered sordid and disgusting may in fact be exciting, risky, a life lived to the full on the edge" (Dyer 2002, 6–7). A public face was given to this terminological usurpation by activist groups such as AIDS Coalition to Unleash Power (ACT UP), founded in 1987, and its spin-off faction Queer Nation, begun in 1990. However, the reclamation of the term was much more widespread and spurred by particular intersecting factors.

By the late 1980s, there was a prevalent and pervasive dissatisfaction with the repressive attitudes, morality, and policies instituted and nurtured by the Republican Party, which had been in power since 1981. The atmosphere of the decade had been one that was in many ways reactionary: gains made by antiwar groups and civil rights movements during the 1960s and 1970s had been lost, retracted, outlawed, or overruled in favour of a socially conformist, morally stifling society which decried (and often persecuted) dissent. Homophobia, racism, and sexism were rife and often institutionally sanctioned. Perhaps most importantly, the spread of HIV/AIDS was initially largely ignored by the Republican Party, and was seen by many in power as predominantly affecting society's "unwanted": Black people, intravenous drug users, gay men. (I will return to the subject of HIV/AIDS in considerably more detail in the next chapter.) George H.W. Bush's election as successor to Ronald Reagan in 1989 marks a particular crisis point. Many queer people felt that expressing dissent had become a fundamental necessity. As Cherry Smyth puts it, the word "queer" marked "a growing lack of faith in the institutions of the state, in political procedures, in the press, the education system, policing and the law" (Smyth 1992, 20).

One marked result of this dissatisfaction was the formation of a number of new activist political groups that used "queer" as a form of self-nomination in their rhetoric and publicity, such as Queer Nation. These groups framed their political approaches and agendas as distinct from those of prior gay rights organisations, such as the Gay Activists Alliance (founded in 1969). Where earlier groups might seek law reform, following legitimate avenues in attempts to secure equal access to institutions such as marriage or the armed forces, queer rights groups chose direct action tactics (demonstrations, graffiti, media interventions) to highlight their distinctive experiences as marginalized people. As Simon Watney puts it, the difference of opinion was "between those who think of the politics of sexuality as a matter of securing minority rights and those who are contesting the overall validity and authenticity of the epistemology of sexuality itself" (Watney 1991, 17). Not, of course, that queer political organisations ousted, killed off, or replaced older lesbian and gay rights activist groups, or that activists could not simultaneously be members of both factions.

Similarly, the term "queer" did not supplant "lesbian and gay." However, the blossoming of queer politics in the late 1980s and early 1990s incorporated the recognition that individual identity labels are always insufficient to capture the messiness and complexity of any one individual's identity – an identity which, moreover, may be susceptible to change over time. As Donald Hall suggests, "queer" means "to abrade the classifications, to sit athwart conventional categories or traverse several" (Hall 2003, 13). Or as

Smyth writes, each use of the word "queer" "defines a strategy, an attitude, a reference to other identities and a new self-understanding" (Smyth 1992, 20). Indeed, "queer" has a certain definitional looseness to it which can be seen as one of its strengths: "part of its political efficacy," writes Annamarie Jagose, "depends on its resistance to definition, and the way in which it refuses to stake its claim" (Jagose 1996, 1).

Temporally lagging slightly behind the advent of queer politics and activism, queer theory emerged as a "new" field of academic enquiry in the early 1990s. The term's first appearance is usually attributed to Teresa de Lauretis, who edited a special issue of the feminist journal *differences* in 1991 with the title "Queer Theory: Lesbian and Gay Sexualities." The use of the phrase "queer theory" was intended, she wrote, to overcome the limitations of terms such as "gay and lesbian," "to avoid all of these fine distinctions in our discursive protocols, not to adhere to any one of the given terms, not to assume their ideological liabilities, but instead to transgress and transcend them – or at the very least problematize them" (de Lauretis 1991, v). The issue's essays covered a range of disparate topics (including the constitution of queer identities in the Global South, queer historiography, and lesbian fetishism) that suggested the scope for future "queer theorizations."

Very swiftly after this volume appeared, queer theory proliferated, through conferences, journal issues, edited collections, and monographs. Reflecting on this material at the end of the decade, Tamsin Spargo summarizes the field:

> Queer theory is not a singular or systematic conceptual or methodological framework, but a collection of intellectual engagements with the relations between sex, gender and sexual desire. If queer theory is a school of thought, then it's one with a highly unorthodox view of discipline. The term describes a diverse range of critical practices and priorities: readings of the representation of same-sex desire in literary texts, films, music, images; analyses of the social and political power relations of sexuality; critiques of the sex-gender system; studies of transsexual and

transgender identification, of sadomasochism and of transgressive desires. (Spargo 1999, 9)

In the intervening years, queer theory has significantly broadened its range of interests and objects of interrogation. Indeed, it has become a scholarly field and a critical arsenal of tools solidly entrenched in the academy.

Throughout all queer theoretical research and argument, however, the field remains centrally concerned with understandings and interrogations of non-normative, contra-heterosexual identities. Whereas lesbian and gay theoretical writings mostly work with an essentialist understanding of identity, of homosexuality as something natural and innate, queer theory is rooted in a constructionist approach. As Donald Hall puts it, queer theories "work to challenge and undercut any attempt to render 'identity' singular, fixed, or normal" (Hall 2003, 15). (This distinction can also be mapped on to that between lesbian and gay activism and queer activism, as Watney suggests above). Michel Foucault's multi-volume work *The History of Sexuality* and Judith Butler's *Gender Trouble* were vital influences on the burgeoning field of queer theory. Foucault challenges binary modes of thought, and identifies homosexuality as a socially and culturally constructed invention of the late 1800s. Butler, wary of the ways in which identity categories are ordered and controlled by those in positions of power, argues that we are compelled to repetitively, compulsively perform gendered roles so that the state will recognise us as legitimate subjects. This performativity provides us with a phantasmatic sense of subjectivity, which covers over a hollow core. As she famously puts it in a 1991 essay, "*gender is a kind of imitation for which there is no original*; in fact, it is a kind of imitation that produces the very notion of an original as an effect and consequence of the imitation itself" (Butler 1991, 21, italics original). This understanding of gender performativity also unsettles stable understandings of categories of sexuality. Though much-debated since, the writings of Foucault and Butler spurred scholars of queer politics and culture to reflect on their ingrained beliefs and understandings of how sexuality and sexual identities form and operate.

When Rich writes that New Queer Cinema made a clean break from "older humanist approaches and the films and tapes that accompanied identity politics," emphasising "social constructionism," she aligns the movement with new strains of queer activism and theory. In a 1993 interview with *Gay Times* magazine, Araki explicitly articulates his queer politics, and specifically critiques more conventional (or gay) approaches to depicting sexually dissident lives:

> I give no apologies for the queerness of my films. I want them to show that I'm a part of a subculture within a subculture, in which the gay community has had us marginalised as we've been influenced by the alternative punk culture … All my films, *Living End* especially, play to the hip, alternative gay and het crowd as opposed to mainstream gays. *Torch Song Trilogy* [1988] and *Longtime Companion* [1989] were alienating movies to me; they didn't move me in any special way. They appeal to a whole different class of people with different values. (Reynolds 1993, 33)

Despite this avowal, *The Living End* is arguably Araki's gayest film, rather than his queerest. In his previous two features, *Three Bewildered People in the Night* (1987) and *The Long Weekend (O' Despair)* (1989), sexuality was somewhat flexible: in the latter, for example, Michael's boyfriend Alex ends up sleeping with Michael's best friend Sara. In contrast, the homo identities of Jon and Luke are never in question. There are also throwaway jokes in *The Living End* which seemed retrograde, gay-male catty, at the time of its release: Luke's snub of Daisy and Fern's lesbian music taste ("Don't these wenches listen to anything but Michelle Shocked and k.d. lang?"), Barbie's dismissal of her husband's bisexuality ("It's not the '70s anymore, when being married to a bisexual was fashionable"). The character of Darcy, Jon's best friend, has been criticised by a number of writers and reviewers for her limited role as emotional support prop. Kimberly Yutani, for instance, refers to her as the "ultimate fag hag," whose "presence is disruptive and intrusive to the main, 'real' story of the boys" (Yutani 1994, 89).

And yet the film is also clearly queer. Its politics, as I unpack in detail in the next chapter, are specifically driven by anger at the HIV/AIDS epidemic that was afflicting gay men and others. In contradistinction to the naturalism and conventionality of "gay cinema," there is a reflexivity to *The Living End* which draws attention on a number of occasions to the fact that we are watching a movie, for instance through performances quoting moments from other films. Further, the stylisation of the world beyond Luke and Jon's and Darcy and Peter's bubbles is patent: as I note in this book's introduction, the secondary characters are largely marked by exaggeration and surreality, played hyperbolically. This is a performance style recognisable from films by antecedent queer underground filmmakers: Andy Warhol, Jack Smith, George Kuchar, John Waters. Peripheral characters are revealed as constructions, their theatricality evident; this reflects onto the other four, inviting us to question why the register of their characterisation, the ways in which they are played, reads as more natural or realistic. *The Living End* may contain prominent gay elements, then, but it is very much a product of its queer moment.

The Positive Images Debate

In 1992, the year that Rich's New Queer Cinema essay was published and *The Living End* entered cinemas, the opening film of the Cannes Film Festival was *Basic Instinct*. The production and release of *Basic Instinct* were met with considerable controversy: for many queer cultural commentators and activists, in its depiction of Catherine Tramell (Sharon Stone), a bisexual novelist who is ultimately revealed to be an ice pick-wielding murderer, the film conflated "perverse" sexuality and homicidal impulses. *Basic Instinct* was seen by some as the latest high-profile example of mainstream cinema reiterating the notion that "deviant" sexuality produces, leads to, or is in some inextricable way affiliated with the desire or need to kill. As such, it seemed to perpetuate a historical lineage that includes such examples as *Rebecca* (1940), *Rope* (1948), *Psycho* (1960), *Freebie and the Bean* (1974), and *Dressed to Kill* (1980). Angela Galvin identifies *Basic Instinct* as extending this representational schema: "The history of lesbians in mainstream film has been a history of moustachioed murderesses and suicides," she writes. "The novelty of *Basic Instinct* may well lie in our heroine's absence of facial hair" (Galvin 1994, 230).

Basic Instinct's problems began relatively early in its production. In February 1991, a copy of the script by Joe Eszterhas leaked and found its way into the hands of a number of gay and queer political groups: the Gay and Lesbian Alliance against Defamation (GLAAD), Queer Nation, ACT UP. A meeting of a dozen activists took place in West Hollywood, with the assembled group voicing their concerns about the planned characterisation of Tramell, as well as the inclusion of a date-rape scene. Responses were swift: members of several gay, queer, and feminist groups sent faxes to 250 newspapers, criticising the negative representation of queerness in the as-yet-not-filmed movie. On 10 April 1991, Queer Nation held a demonstration at a location that was being prepared for some exterior shooting. As Stevie Simkin writes, "Over the following weeks, [pressure groups] stepped up their action, picketing locations and shouting and chanting to try and cause maximum disruption to cast and crew. The impact of the protests on the progress of the production was considerable … Some temporary sets were daubed with paint, necessitating a shift of location and redecoration; cables were cut and protesters flashed torches at the cameras during filming" (Simkin 2013, 31). On 24 April, a meeting was held at a San Francisco Hyatt between activists and members of the film's creative team: Eszterhas, director Paul Verhoeven, and producer Alan Marshall. Members of several political organisations attended: National Organization for Women, Community United against Violence, Queer Nation, and ACT UP. The intention was to air grievances and to reach a resolution.

The pressure groups demanded script changes, even suggesting that the lead character, detective Nick Curran (Michael Douglas), should be recast as a woman. Eszterhas offered to make some alterations to the script, but the film's production company Carolco rejected this opportunity. It subsequently issued an official statement, saying that the changes proposed by the protesters "undermine the strength of Eszterhas's original material, weaken the characters ... and lessen the integrity of the picture itself" (Lyons 1997, 129, ellipsis original). The picketing continued, with demonstrators chanting and blowing whistles attempting to disrupt the film's production. On one occasion, Marshall succeeded in getting the police to arrest around thirty demonstrators.

When *Basic Instinct* opened in cinemas in the spring of 1992, queer groups and National Organization for Women members protested in front of cinemas in Los Angeles, San Francisco, New York, Seattle, Washington, DC, and other cities. The largest gatherings were in San Francisco. Demonstrators handed out leaflets, blew whistles, and carried placards with slogans such as "Hollywood Promotes Anti-Gay Violence" and (a major spoiler) "Save Your Money – The Bisexual Did It." Despite the protests, *Basic Instinct* was a major commercial hit, becoming one of the top-grossing studio films of the year (figure 7). Reviews from critics were mixed, and it is especially notable that queer writers differed in their opinions. In NYQ, Michael Bronski wrote that "*Basic Instinct* is a symbol of how deep is popular culture's hatred of queers and women, and its director's and producer's refusal to take seriously our criticism testifies to how little power we wield in this society" (Lyons 1997, 145). In contrast, Rich appeared on the BBC's *Late Show* and argued that lesbians "with a sense of humour" would enjoy the film. In a 1993 essay, she even suggests that queer activists who campaigned against *Basic Instinct* might have had ulterior motives: "For queers as for anyone else, it's a lot of fun to attack Hollywood, mingle by association with the frustratingly withheld objects of desire, and pick up the extra media mileage that glitz-by-association bestows" (Rich 1993, 84). As this discrepancy between critical perspectives reveals, some queer audience members were unconcerned about taking pleasure in

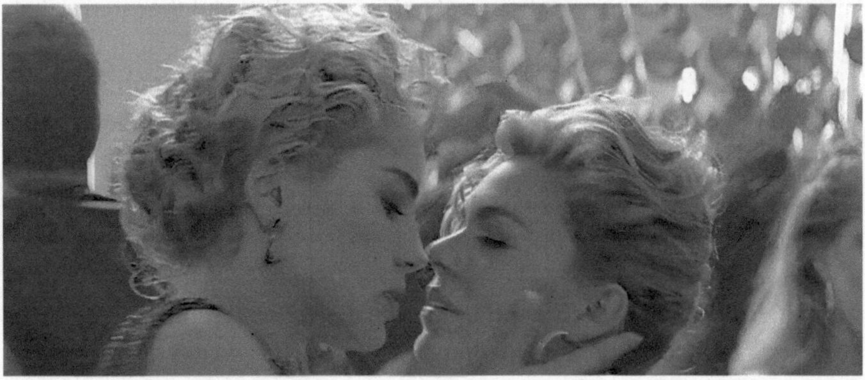

Figure 7
Queer critics disagreed on whether *Basic Instinct* (1992) made troubling use of negative stereotypes, or was sexy entertainment featuring strong women characters.

narratives featuring pejorative stereotypes, setting aside their knowledge of Hollywood's damaging and painful history of misrepresentation. Perhaps the lesbian and gay political push for "positive images" in mainstream media was coming to an end?

The history of that political push needs some unpacking. As the gay rights movement in the United States gathered force across the 1970s, one of the issues that activists confronted was media representations of lesbian and gay individuals. Historically, when Hollywood cinema depicted queer characters, it did so through subtle coding and stereotypes (the sissy, the butch dyke, the sad young man), emphasising any derogatory aspects. In June 1973, gay activists sat down with representatives of the film and television industries to raise concerns about the representation of homosexuality on big and small screens. That summer, the Gay Activists Alliance, in collaboration with the National Gay Task Force, authored a set of "General Principles for Motion Picture and Television Treatment of Homosexuality." This document addresses the use of homosexuality as a target of humour, derogatory labels and language, the "naturalness" of gay and lesbian sexuality, and the interrelatedness of marginalized rights struggles. The fourth of the eight guidelines, while acknowledging that "stereotypical people do exist," argues that "until a broad spectrum of the gay community is expressed on film and the stereotypes are put into perspective, their use is damaging" (Russo 1987, 220–1). Without using the phrase, the guidelines call for positive images of homosexuality on film and television; they echo similar concerns expressed by other activists and organisations regarding how the mainstream media has historically depicted women, people of colour, and other marginalized populations.

Across the 1970s and 1980s, theoretical and critical writings by lesbian and gay writers wrangled with mainstream cinema's history of denigrating queer characters. In *Gays and Film* (1977), a short book edited by Richard Dyer published to accompany a season of queer films screening at London's National Film Theatre, Dyer himself engages with the problem of stereotypes. There "can be no doubt," he writes, "that most stereotypes of gays in films are demeaning and offensive … The amount of hatred, fear, ridicule and disgust packed into those images is unmistakable." He advocates "understanding just what stereotypes are, how they function, ideologically and aesthetically, and why they are so resilient in the face of our rejection of them" (Dyer 1977, 27). He recognises the value of social types as mental shortcuts, but also the political necessity of "exposing the reactionary political force of most social and stereo-typing" (Dyer 1977, 39). In an essay published in *Jump Cut* in 1981, a group of lesbian writers engage at length with the political complexities of depicting lesbian life on screen. The "economic pressures of marketing and film production," they write, "guarantee that in a homophobic society, any authentic 'positive image' of lesbian romantic love remains too great a risk ever to find direct expression" (Becker et al. 1981, 18). Perhaps most significantly, in his book *The Celluloid Closet*, a survey of Hollywood's depictions of queerness first published in 1981, Vito Russo concludes that "the history of the portrayal of lesbians and gay men in mainstream cinema is politically indefensible and aesthetically revolting … Gay visibility has never really been an issue in the movies. Gays have always been visible. It's *how* they have been visible that has remained offensive for almost a century" (Russo 1987, 235). Against this, he argues the need for "more films that explore people who happen to be gay in America and how their lives intersect with the dominant culture" (Russo 1987, 236). His call is for depictions of quotidian queers, ones whose sexuality is not made into an issue, and he points to independently made films such as *Desert Hearts* (1985) and *Parting Glances* (1986) as evidence that such representations are possible.

The notion of positive imagery, however, is a complex one. As Diane Waldman highlights, one of the central problems is the twofold connotation of the term "positive": it can mean "concerned only with real things and experience; empirical," but it also means "affirmative" or "constructive," "tending in the direction regarded as that of progress" (Waldman 1990, 14). When positive images are discussed, both of these definitions usually come into play: a call for positive images implies a need for more truth, to effect a political corrective. This is evident in Richard Dyer's take, in his book *Now You See It*, on what constitutes "positive imagery": "Positive meant three, not altogether incompatible things: thereness, insisting on the fact of our existence; goodness, asserting our worth and that of our life-styles; and realness, showing what we were in fact like" (Dyer 2003, 254). The emphasis Dyer places on the morally inflected "goodness" of positive images highlights their political dimensions. But why should a positive image automatically be a good one? As the *Jump Cut* essay writers acknowledged in 1981, "positive images, like negative images, suppress contradiction and are thus static" (Becker et al 1981, 18).

Clare Whatling offers a sustained analysis of the positive images debate in her book *Screen Dreams*. She poses fundamental queries: For whom are these images positive? Whose life do they represent? The types and variety of positive images of queerness available and allowable is, she suggests, already politically prescribed in advance: "Positive for whom is not merely a question of personal taste but a political question raised within a context where some people's sexuality is still more acceptable than others" (Whatling 1997, 84).

For his part, Ellis Hanson argues that the notion of positive images as more "accurate" and "truthful" – what Waldman identifies as their relationship to the empirical – raises a host of interrelated questions regarding queer representation and spectatorship:

> What is the truth of homosexuality? Whose experience is genuine and whose is merely a stereotype? Why valorize verisimilitude over fantasy in works of art? Why suppose that anyone would like homosexuals more if they could see them the way they really are? Does the reality of gay people's lives necessarily make for good cinema? If someone made a movie about *my* life, I doubt I would go to see it. (Hanson 1999, 8)

By the 1990s, then, queer commentators were scrutinising the "goodness" or "rightness" of positive images of sexually dissident characters, with films such as *Basic Instinct* serving as a spur in the articulation of diverging perspectives.

So, too, did New Queer Cinema. A number of films under its umbrella offer an explicit provocation to the "positive images" drive, with the key titles being *Poison*, *Swoon*, and *The Living End*. All three of these films, as Michele Aaron notes, "beautify the criminal and (homo)eroticise violence" (Aaron 2004, 4). In each, pejorative stereotypes are afforded diegetic prominence, challenging queer audiences (and others) to reconsider their relationship to cinema's representational politics. *Swoon* provides a useful point of contrast with *The Living End*: the first feature by Tom Kalin, it re-tells the story of eighteen-year-olds Nathan Leopold and Richard Loeb, who in 1924 kidnapped and murdered fourteen-year-old Bobby Franks. The couple were arrested and sentenced to life in prison. This true-life tale had previously been the basis for the films *Rope* (1948) and *Compulsion* (1959), but *Swoon* was the first to make explicit the sexual relationship that existed between the two murderers. Shot in crisp black and white, the film includes theatrical flourishes, playful anachronisms, and moments of surrealism, but it is also informed by significant research into the facts of the case (figure 8). Rich, in her original "New Queer Cinema"

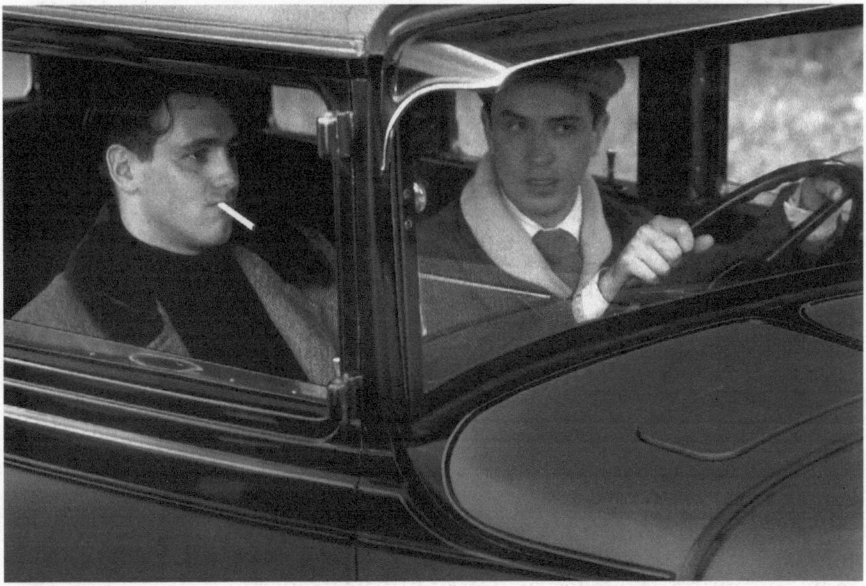

Figure 8
Daniel Schlachet and Craig Chester as real-life murderers Loeb and Leopold in Tom Kalin's *Swoon* (1992), a film which B. Ruby Rich argues invites us to "claim the heroes, claim the villains" (Rich 1992, 34).

essay, highlights the fact that Kalin's film "demonstrates how easily mainstream society of the '20s could unite discrete communities of outsiders (Jews, queers, Blacks, murderers) into a commonality of perversion." She hopes the film will provoke a "rethinking" of the positive images debate, and argues it is time to "claim the heroes, claim the villains, and don't mistake any of it for realness" (Rich 1992, 34). As Kalin himself puts it, "We're in a sorry state if we can't afford to look at 'unwholesome' lesbian or gay people … It's dangerous if we can't speak from within our own communities about issues that are politically problematic. [Positive representation] has its place because it represents many lives, but it doesn't represent my desires" (Okewole 1992, 37).

The Living End also traffics in "unwholesome" queer characterisation. Here it is worth detailing the litany of crimes Luke and Jon commit – the evidence that would brand them as negative role models for queer audiences. Luke operates most obviously outside of and against the law. The film opens with him committing a minor offence, spray-painting graffiti (a regular habit, it seems: he later uses a marker to write "I Blame Society" on a concrete pillar, alters the wording of homophobic bathroom scrawl, and pens "Jon + Luke Till Death Do Us Part" on a phonebooth wall). He purloins Daisy and Fern's car, though in this case he was being threatened with a gun and needed to escape. He shoots three homophobes in what could be seen as self-defence, although he may have been able to scare them off without resorting to murder. Off screen, he kills a cop (or thinks he did: "I mean, it's not like I stopped to check his pulse or anything"). His bludgeoning of a neo-Nazi with a boombox is battery and assault, though provoked by the fascist's homophobic remarks ("adios, infected dick suckers"). His shooting of an ATM, arguably brought on by frustration, is the destruction of private property.

Jon at no point carries out any similar sorts of physical violence or property damage. He and Luke both go shopping with a stolen credit card. Although Luke says that it belongs to a friend, his uncle, Jon clearly knows it is pilfered ("I think we ought to at least feel a little guilty," he says). Jon's greatest crime, arguably, is not reporting Luke to the police: though he repeatedly grows frustrated with Luke, he never calls in the authorities. Neither does Darcy, for that matter, who must have some knowledge of Luke's behaviour. In fact, the police are nowhere to be seen in *The Living End*: there are no scenes of detective footwork, no high-speed pursuit. Their only brief appearance is a flash: at one point on their travels, while Luke is giving Jon a blowjob in the moving car, Jon spots a patrol vehicle parked by the side of the road, and jolts. (The absence of the police in the film may have been a budgetary concern: how much would renting a police uniform and/or car have added to the film's costs?) Of course, the broader landscape in which the narrative of *The Living End* takes place is one marked by madness, violence, and lawlessness: psychotic female killers who describe their previous murders in gleeful detail; jealous wives who murder their spouses with knives; sparring couples quickly provoked to verbal assault; groups of homophobic vigilantes. The version of Los Angeles in which much of the film takes place is a contemporary incarnation of the Wild West, where individuals have to fend for themselves and societal norms are breaking down.

Araki claims that *The Living End* was "so controversial and divisive when it came out – people were telling me stories about fistfights breaking out in bars over it" (Smith 2008). However, any ire it incited amongst queer audiences and community members was negligible compared to that provoked by *Basic Instinct*. Underlying the distinction between the queer responses to these films are suppositions about the reach and potential impact of mainstream cinema compared with its independent counterpart – including problematic assumptions about the abilities of differing audiences to distinguish fiction from reality, and to remain unaffected by negative portrayals of marginalized people. Some instances of New Queer Cinema may have broken past the queer niche audience, but their creators were not making films for a broader demographic and were unconcerned about trafficking in unwholesome depictions of queer characters. As Tom Kalin argues, "I think the solution is to make more images rather than less; if someone hates [*Swoon*], they should make something that counters it" (Okewole 1992, 37).

Independent Cinema

For Rich, 1992 was "a watershed year for independent gay and lesbian film and video" (Rich 1992, 31). Here, I want to emphasise Rich's use of the word "independent" and to dwell on its ramifications. *The Living End*'s appearance in cinemas coincided with, and was part of, a significant boom in independent American film that had been occurring for a few years. In addition to being the high watermark year for New Queer Cinema, 1992 was also a significant year for US independent film more broadly, with the release of, amongst others, *Daughters of the Dust*, *Gas Food Lodging*, *Simple Men*, *In the Soup*, *Bad Lieutenant*, and *Reservoir Dogs*. A number of commentators discuss Araki's film in relation to financial, aesthetic, and institutional discourses of independence, articulating the significance of his film as both queer *and* independent. Indeed, although Rich paid attention in her original essay to a smattering of lesbian works on video, it is arguable that the pivotal films identified with New Queer Cinema are all independent features. The "emergence of an American independent cinema," Rich later wrote, was "the fertile ground from which the New Queer Cinema [would] leap" (Rich 2013, 6). Examining *The Living End*'s status as an independent film can provide valuable insights into the ways in which it was discussed, promoted, and framed – and the wider cinematic landscape into which it slotted.

"Independence" in American cinema has always been, as Chuck Kleinhans articulates, "a relational term – independent in relation to the dominant system – rather than ... a practice that is totally free-standing and autonomous" (Kleinhans 1998, 308). Ever since the studio system calcified into a bloc composed of several prominent market leaders – that is, since the 1920s – independent forms of cinema production have operated beyond its walls. Over the last century, the label "independent cinema" has been affixed to an extremely diverse array of films, with its meaning shifting and mutating. As Yannis Tzioumakis writes, independent film is perhaps best understood as "a discourse that expands and contracts when socially authorised institutions (filmmakers, industry practitioners, trade publications, academics, film critics, and so on) contribute towards its definition at different periods in the history of American cinema" (Tzioumakis 2006, 11). Thus, it has been used to refer to B-movies and genre pics produced by companies such as Monogram and Republic in the 1930s; to exploitation films aimed at teenagers made by organisations such as American Independent Pictures in the 1950s; to work by members of the "New American Cinema," such as John Cassavetes and Shirley Clarke, in the early 1960s; and to much more besides. The relationship between independent film production and the Hollywood studios is often blurred, with many titles produced outside the oligarchy financially supported and/or distributed by the majors. (Ironically, *Basic Instinct* can even be seen as independent, in that its production company Carolco operated outside of the studio system.) In recent decades, the industrial distinction between mainstream and independent production has become increasingly complex, with the growth of studio boutique and arthouse labels, the rise to prominence of streaming and production platforms such as Amazon and Netflix, and the critical and financial success of nominally independent companies such as A24.

In the 1980s, however, a number of factors fostered a vibrant independent film scene in the United States. The generation of directors that began making films during that decade grew up during the 1960s and 1970s, an era when America's film culture altered significantly. The films available to see in cinemas diversified to include a much broader array of global cinema and "alternative" titles. Film schools and university courses devoted to teaching cinema began to proliferate; prior to this, filmmaking training had largely been restricted to apprenticeships within the studios. In addition, the Hollywood system was temporarily transformed by the "New Hollywood" films of directors such as George Lucas, Francis Ford Coppola, Robert Altman, Terrence Malick, and Arthur Penn – all directors invested in reformatting genre cinema with hints of an arthouse or experimental sensibility. It is clear how these factors affected Araki's career: he studied film theory and film practice at university; he had formative encounters with European cinema as a young man; his films, perhaps influenced by "New Hollywood" approaches, have often perverted standard genres (road movie, teen film, romantic comedy).

From the 1970s into the 1980s, the industrial infrastructure necessary to support the production and distribution of independent cinema began to fall into place. Several new small distribution companies (such as the Samuel Goldwyn Company, founded in 1978) were established. The Independent Feature Film Market and the Sundance Film Festival became key sites for the development of new work. A substantial enlargement in exhibition opportunities occurred through an increase in the number of cinema screens, the boom in home video, and the expansion of cable TV; all generated a demand for films to show. Reagan's economic policies of the 1980s also helped. As Geoff King notes, under the President's reforms, "investment capital was made available for film production and distribution while consumer expenditure also increased … A range of financial mechanisms, including loans, grants, limited partnerships and public offerings, were available to filmmakers" (King 2005, 23). At the same time, the conservatism of the Hollywood studios in the late 1970s and 1980s led audiences to desire a more diverse diet of film offerings, a broader buffet. There were a number of notable independent critical and/or commercial successes in the early-to-mid 1980s, including *Chan Is Missing* (1982), *Smithereens* (1982), *Stranger than Paradise* (1984), and *She's Gotta Have It* (1986). For John Pierson, the year that marked the high watermark for independent cinema was 1989, when Steven Soderbergh's *sex, lies, and videotape* won the Palme d'Or at the Cannes Film Festival (Pierson 1996).

King argues that independent films are usually marked by particular factors: their "industrial location," "the kinds of formal and aesthetic strategies they adopt," and "their relationship to the broader social, cultural, political or ideological landscape" (King 2005, 2). Sherry Ortner, whilst recognising that independent films exist on a spectrum, argues that such works are marked by their "relatively low budgets," "often set out to challenge their viewers with relatively 'difficult' subject matter and/or techniques," "are often explicitly political and critical," and (in contrast to Hollywood investment in fantasy) "are usually highly realist" and avoid happy endings (Ortner 2013, 4). Here, partly drawing on these perspectives, I want to briefly unpack three facets of *The Living End* that have been used to position or identify it as independent: (a) its extremely small budget; (b) Araki's networked connections with an array of film industry personnel who were largely operating beyond the studio system; and (c) political connections between queer independent film and independent work from other marginalized and subaltern directors.

As I noted in this book's introduction, *The Living End* was made for a very low sum of money: $22,769. The film became a key case study in pieces of writing by Peter Broderick for *Filmmaker Magazine*, alongside Robert Rodriguez's *El Mariachi* ($7,225) and Nick Gomez's *Laws of Gravity* ($38,000). Micro-budget independent films had been made previously, of course: *The Return of the Secaucus Seven* (1980) cost around $60,000; *Chan Is Missing* $22,000. However, these three films released in the same year were all made with an extreme economy of means. Broderick connects together their creators: "These filmmakers embodied a radically different approach to filmmaking … They rejected the old model which required finding financing from third parties. This had long been the paradigm given the high cost of moviemaking … They assessed their resources first, and then wrote scripts which utilized them … Their projects didn't require money from strangers. This allowed them to devote their time and energy to writing, rehearsing, and making their movies rather than chasing financing" (Broderick 2002). On these micro-budget films, equipment was often borrowed, and cast and crew worked for free, providing their own props and costumes. As King puts it, "Production at this end of the spectrum can have the appearance of something closer to a non-industrial, home-movie enterprise" (King 2005, 13). Certainly, a familial atmosphere sometimes dominated proceedings on *The Living End*: producer Marcus Hu's mother cooked chop suey for the cast and crew. The tiny cost of Araki's film became one of the ways in which it was promoted, a hook for journalists and audiences: just as Rodriguez repeatedly mentioned that $7,000 figure, Araki often brought up his film's budget – but highlighted that $22,000 is a lot of money when you have already made two films which each cost just $5,000.

By 1992, Araki had been making films for several years and had established a substantial network of collaborators and allies. Unsurprisingly, one limb of that network connected a group of queer filmmakers. In addition, and overlapping with the queer grouping, Araki was linked into a broader ecology of independent cinema practitioners. On the West Coast of the United States, Araki and Gus Van Sant's lives intersected as they tried to launch their respective careers: Araki sent experimental and poetic letters to Van Sant; Van Sant remembers sitting in a palazzo with Araki in 1987 in Italy when both had films screening in the Torino Gay and Lesbian Film Festival ("Pioneers" 2022). The character of Gus in *The Living End* – who Jon and Luke visit in San Francisco – is named after Van Sant. One of the three homophobes Luke shoots wears a *Drugstore Cowboy* T-shirt not as a snub of its director Van Sant, but because the associate producer of *The Living End*, Andrea Sperling, had been an intern at the production company Avenue Pictures and had nabbed some swag ("Pioneers" 2022). The individual responsible for the lighting on *The Living End* was Christopher Münch; raised and based on the West Coast, like Araki, Münch was working on his own debut during the making of Araki's film. *The Hours and Times* (1991) – at sixty minutes probably better defined as a short than a feature – offers a speculative account of what might have happened between John Lennon (Ian Hart) and Brian Epstein (David Angus) during a sojourn to Barcelona in 1963. In January 1992, Münch's film was part of the wave of new queer films that screened at Sundance, where it won a Special Jury Recognition award.

Other personnel involved in the making of *The Living End* reveal some of the broader independent cinema networks with which Araki was connected at the time. Jon Jost and Henry Rosenthal were two of the film's four executive producers. Rosenthal was the producer of Jost's *All the Vermeers in New York* and *Sure Fire* (both 1990). After *The Living End*, he went on to produce further films by Jost, *Frameup* (1993) and *The Bed You Sleep In* (1993), as well as Jon Moritsugu's *Mod Fuck Explosion* (1994). (Jost and Rosenthal have cameo appearances in Moritsugu's film, which Andrea Sperling co-produced.) *The Living End*'s co-producer was Jim Stark, who had been working with

Jim Jarmusch as co-producer of *Down by Law* (1986), producer of *Mystery Train* (1989), and executive producer of *Night on Earth* (1991); he was also the producer of Alexandre Rockwell's film *In the Soup*. After the release of *The Living End*, according to Araki, Stark said to him, "You make these gay movies that gay people hate … If you make a straight movie, I'll produce it and get you real money for it." Araki agreed, and Stark signed up as an associate producer of *The Doom Generation*, a film announced in its opening credits as "A Heterosexual Movie by Gregg Araki." The director now refers to it as a "super queer, ostensibly straight movie" (Dry 2022). Stark has not worked with Araki again.

Araki evidently sees himself as part of a wider independent cinema movement of the late 1980s and early 1990s. He often refers to himself as a "film nerd" and uses this concept to forge a link with his filmmaker peers: "My generation, like me and Gus [Van Sant] and Quentin [Tarantino] and Rick Linklater, even if some of us didn't go to formal film school, we're all so steeped in that language and that history" (Dry 2022). Journalists make similar connections. Writing in *Sight and Sound* about *The Living End* and *Swoon*, for instance, Amy Taubin relates these films to *Reservoir Dogs* and *Laws of Gravity*, due to their depictions of brutality: "Like Tarantino and Gomez, Araki and Kalin are also the sons of Scorsese, whose films define and critique masculinity through violence but also make Robert De Niro a homoerotic object of desire" (Taubin 1992). Linklater arguably makes for a more apposite point of comparison. As identified in the introduction to this book, he contributed to *The Living End*, shooting driving footage in Texas. In a 2023 conversation between Araki and Linklater, they discuss their shared obsessive urge, early in their careers, to make cinema. As Araki states: "That's why we're all friends and there's this network of us today, because when we meet each other, it's your tribe. You know what I mean? You're like, 'Oh, we're the same. We're all crazy. We're all just obsessed with filmmaking' … We're all the same level of freak, and we all have the same battle stories of like, 'Oh, yeah, remember that day the camera fell out of the car and somebody died?'" (King-Clements 2023). Araki and Linklater's films are markedly different. However, both men began their careers with low-budget work that caught the attention of a wider industry and audience and established them as directors with distinctive voices.

Independent cinema is often characterised as expressing a radical or dissenting point of view, and/or as providing a channel of expression for marginalized individuals (queers, women, people of colour, and so on) who would otherwise struggle to get their stories told by the mainstream. As Sherry Ortner puts it, independent films "are in the business of 'cultural critique,' going up against the dominant culture by way of being 'not Hollywood'" (Ortner 2013, 10). Of course, independent productions can be just as conservative, heteronormative, sexist, and racist as mainstream cinema. However, a lower budget and more creative freedom can forge opportunities to voice alternative perspectives. Araki is both a queer filmmaker and an Asian American filmmaker; for a number of commentators, his work requires positioning in regard to both queer and Asian American independent fields of film production. Daryl Chin, for instance, suggests that Araki's work should not only be situated in relation to work by Todd Haynes, Su Friedrich, Peggy Ahwesh, and Gus Van Sant, but also to films by Roddy Bogawa, Trinh T. Minh-ha, and Jon Moritsugu (Chin 1993, 107). Araki wrote a short essay for a 1991 book on independent Asian Pacific American media arts, entitled "The (Sorry) State of (Independent) Things," in which he discusses his status as a member of two different marginalized communities. He is worth quoting at length:

> As a gay Asian American, I consider myself a card-carrying (albeit controversial) member of two, count 'em two, "oppressed" subcultural groups, and I've been screened on the circuit under both "umbrellas." While, like any struggling independent, I'm always grateful to have my work shown/seen/discussed, I've found that the response to my films

> within those contingents is often, surprisingly, more hostile and xenophobic than even that of the Mainstream … Lackadaisical conformity and formulaic toeing of the "politically correct" line are celebrated by audiences, critics and programmers alike. Like Paramount and Universal, the so-called "Other" Cinemas have gotten lazy, complacent and retrogressive in their outlook. (Araki 1991, 69)

Here, Araki expresses his dissatisfaction with normative subcultural politics, with the "political correctness" that produces positive images (of sexuality, of gender, of race). His identity may align him with communities of queer filmmakers and Asian American filmmakers, but his independent stance sets him at odds with both.

In this chapter, I have introduced, and reflected on, the New Queer Cinema moment of the late 1980s and early 1990s – a moment of which *The Living End* was a key part. In particular, I have scrutinised the queerness of New Queer Cinema and of Araki's film, identified the ways in which *The Living End* played a role in the debate about positive images of queer lives and experiences that was especially charged in the early 1990s, and situated Araki and his work in relation to discourses of independence. What I have only touched on so far is the role that HIV/AIDS played in giving birth to New Queer Cinema, and the ways in which the films associated with the movement engaged with it. It is to this topic that I now turn.

Chapter 2

Retroviral Cinema

New Queer Cinema's flourishing in the early 1990s occurred after a decade of HIV infections and AIDS deaths, at a time when effective treatment against HIV was still being sought. The first cases of a new illness were detected in 1981, when a number of gay men presented with particular symptoms (Kaposi's sarcoma, pneumocystis carinii pneumonia) in major cities including Los Angeles, New York, and San Francisco. Though initially the disease was known as gay-related immunodeficiency (GRID) and as the "4H disease" (as the main groups affected seemed to be homosexuals, heroin users, haemophiliacs, and Haitians), it was labelled acquired immunodeficiency syndrome (AIDS) by the Centers for Disease Control in 1982. A retrovirus, which attacks the immune system and makes it susceptible to an array of opportunistic infections, was identified as the cause of AIDS in 1984; after being known by various names, it was officially called "human immunodeficiency virus (HIV)" in 1986. The virus spread swiftly, and the demographics it impacted shifted over the years. In 1992, the year of release for *The Living End*, AIDS became the number one cause of death for US men aged 25 to 44. The annual number of deaths from AIDS in the United States peaked at 41,699 in 1995. In 1996, the discovery of effective combination therapies allowed many of those infected with HIV, for the first time, to no longer see it as a fatal condition.

In the early 1980s, when it was not yet clear how HIV is transmitted, misinformation and fearmongering were rife. Due to its initial manifestations in gay communities, many saw AIDS as a "gay disease" and homosexual men as sources of contagion. Governmental responses to the epidemic in the United States were marked by lethargy and homophobia. President Ronald Reagan only gave his first speech about AIDS in 1987, in it calling for immigrants and prisoners to undergo mandatory HIV testing. Reagan's administration opposed bills that would prevent discrimination against those with AIDS. In 1987, Congress passed the Helms Amendment, which prohibited using federal funding for any AIDS education or prevention materials that "promote, encourage, or condone homosexual activities." It was this climate – of political neglect, rising numbers of HIV infections and deaths related to complications from AIDS, slow responses from the medical establishment, and vilification of people with HIV and AIDS from all quarters – that led to the formation of several direct-action queer activist groups, including the AIDS Coalition to Unleash Power (ACT UP) and Gran Fury.

ACT UP, founded in New York in March 1987, was in its own words, "a diverse, nonpartisan group of individuals, united in anger and committed to direct action to end the AIDS crisis" (Schulman 2021, v). Subsequently, other chapters of the group formed in cities across the United States, as well as in London, Berlin, and Paris. ACT UP's genesis is often traced to a fiery speech given by writer and activist Larry Kramer, in which he castigates the Gay Men's Health Crisis for its lack of political action, criticises New York's health care system, and lays into the Food and Drug Administration's protracted approval processes, which were affecting the potential availability of AIDS treatments. His speech fired up the crowd and led, two days later, to the formation of ACT UP; its first demonstration took place a fortnight after. ACT UP's public and disruptive activities were attention-grabbing, and included activists breaking into the New York Stock Exchange and chaining themselves to a balcony to protest the cost of HIV/AIDS drug azidothymidine (AZT); a large-scale die-in in St Patrick's Cathedral, New York, spurred by the church's stance on homosexuality, abortion, and safer sex; and a group breaking into a CBS studio during a live news broadcast to promote fighting AIDS.

The impact and dissemination of queer political activism in the late 1980s in the United States was facilitated by a striking and sophisticated use of slogans and graphic imagery. The graphic emblem "silence = death," white type under a pink triangle on a black background, became a defining symbol of queer activism of the time (and, due to its effectiveness, has persisted).[1] Its creation preceded the formation of ACT UP, whose members adopted it as a central image of their campaigning. As Douglas Crimp and Adam Rolston note, in appropriating the pink triangle used in Nazi concentration camps to mark gay men, "'silence = death' declares that silence about the oppression and annihilation of gay people, then and now, must be broken as a matter of our survival" (Crimp and Rolston 1990, 14). A significant political force working with and alongside ACT UP was the artist collective Gran Fury, which took its name from the New York Police Department's model of car. Some of Gran Fury's activist interventions – bold and direct, with striking juxtapositions of imagery and slogans – have become recognised as significant artworks and subsequently exhibited in galleries. These include: "Read My Lips" posters (1988) used to promote a public kiss-in, which had both "boys" and "girls" iterations, the former using a photograph of sailors kissing taken during World War II, the latter a picture from a 1920s Broadway play featuring a lesbian couple; counterfeit money (1988) which featured photocopied $10, $50, and $100 bills on one side and furious slogans aimed at Wall Street bankers on the reverse (such as "FUCK YOUR PROFITEERING. People are dying while you play business."); and the safer sex slogan "Men: Use Condoms or Beat It" (1988), which was printed on stickers, badges, and T-shirts.[2]

There are direct connections between ACT UP, Gran Fury, and New Queer Cinema – specifically, in relation to the film movement's East Coast faction. Tom Kalin, director of *Swoon*, was a member of both ACT UP and Gran Fury. He says that ACT UP meetings resembled his fantasy of New York socialist communist meetings of the 1930s: "It had that romantic whiff to it because it seemed utterly urgent, completely improvised, totally responsive and nimble, [and] highly intelligent" (Kalin 2004). In 1990, Gran Fury produced four thirty-second public service announcements about AIDS called "Kissing Doesn't Kill." Filmed as parodies of Benetton fashion adverts, they were designed to promote sexual and racial diversity as well as tolerance in relation to HIV/AIDS. For Kalin, this project provided an insight into the power of mass media to get activist messages across to the public: "You need to work to engage in the politics of Michael Jackson, Madonna, Benetton. There is no outside the marketplace in relation to art production" (Juhasz 1995, 59). Todd Haynes was also a member of ACT UP and (briefly) Gran Fury. He recalls ACT UP's extraordinary effectiveness: "That was a case of remarkable and very specific change that happened because of direct political action. It had immediate goals that it succeeded in achieving in an expedient amount of time" (Gilbey 2020). Christine Vachon, who produced both *Swoon* and *Poison*, was in ACT UP, too. Haynes and Vachon, along with Barry Ellsworth, had formed a nonprofit film production company together in 1987 called Apparatus; Gran Fury held its first few meetings in Apparatus's office on Lafayette Street in New York.

In an essay published in 1993, José Arroyo argues that the HIV/AIDS pandemic was the driving force behind New Queer Cinema. AIDS, he writes, "has effected what amounts to an epistemic shift in gay culture": "We know different things about ourselves and we know ourselves differently (and part of this change is a questioning of who is 'we' and what is the self). AIDS is why there is New Queer Cinema and it is what New Queer Cinema is about" (Arroyo 1993, 92). Discussing a number of examples that were shaped indirectly – and occasionally directly – by AIDS, he identifies them all as "attempts to grapple with the ways in which the pandemic has changed our lives" (Arroyo 1993, 93). For B. Ruby Rich, the film movement emerged from a felt urge a decade into the pandemic: "The need was intense for work that could make sense of what was going on, take stock, and reformulate our imaginings, to grieve the dead, yes, but also to reinvigorate life and love and possibility. For gay men, it was a matter of life or death, a question of mortality or immortality. For lesbians, it was a matter of empathy, a horror at what was happening to our/their gay brothers and outrage at society's response" (Rich 2013, xix). New Queer Cinema, she suggests, flourished as the actions and interventions of groups such as ACT UP began to wane, "just when the passionate energy that had characterized AIDS activism was flagging" (Rich 2013, xix). For his part, from his West Coast base, Araki was never involved in any queer political direct action groups. As he told Dale Reynolds: "I'm not particularly political, except in my art; I'm not an activist person. I essentially make movies and buy records" (Reynolds 1993, 34). However, as Arroyo argues, as a key film in the New Queer Cinema pantheon, *The Living End* needs to be situated in the context of the HIV/AIDS pandemic and the activist anger that manifested in the late 1980s and early 1990s. It also requires framing in relation to previous attempts by film- and video-makers to engage with HIV/AIDS. These are my aims in this chapter.

Film, Video, and HIV/AIDS

Before and after the advent of New Queer Cinema, communities of sexual dissidents used film and video in different ways to respond to HIV/AIDS. Activists drew on video's cheapness and immediacy to produce community-oriented tapes that aimed to share resources, promote resilience, and provide a corrective to mainstream mis-messaging. Artists used film and video to engage with the politics as well as the social and cultural ramifications of HIV/AIDS. Yet others attempted to use fictional storytelling to narrate the impact of the epidemic, to humanise those impacted by the virus, and to generate sympathy and understanding. Those using these different modes were in no way isolated from each other, and many film- and video-makers used more than one approach. Here, I want to pay attention to some precursors of New Queer Cinema that engaged with HIV/AIDS, and the ways in which they worked with and/or against its mainstream representations and understandings. I focus in particular on feature-length films made for cinemas, and on several key video works made by artists who were later affiliated with the film movement.

First, though, *An Early Frost* can help to set the stage. A feature-length drama made for television that NBC aired in November 1985, it starred Aidan Quinn as Chicago-based lawyer Michael Pierson who, on discovering he is seropositive, travels to the home of his parents to reveal both his homosexuality and his HIV status. Michael's parents, played by Ben Gazzara and Gena Rowlands, react differently to his news; his mother is more patient and understanding. In hospital, Michael befriends Victor (John Glover), another HIV-positive patient, who subsequently dies. Back at his parents', Michael attempts to kill himself but his father stops him. He ultimately returns to Chicago. *An Early Frost* reached a large demographic of television viewers, providing them with a sustained representation of a gay HIV-positive man – one who experiences bouts of ill health but does not die. However, its gay writers Ron Cowen and Daniel Lipman battled against the restrictions of network television. They had to dilute and balance overtly queer-positive political points with opposing homophobic perspectives; NBC was antsy about depicting any physical contact between Michael and his lover; they had to consult the Centers for Disease Control about whether a casual family kiss between Michael and his grandmother (Sylvia Sidney) could be shown.

Although *An Early Frost* was lauded with awards and award nominations, some queer critics had serious reservations about this mainstream tale. For Vito Russo, the telefilm shows "how AIDS affects a young man's mother, father, sister, brother-in-law and grandmother. There is no consideration given to the fact that this is happening to him – not them … Such films are about the real people in our society, the straight people. Gays are the problem they have" (Russo 1987, 277). Richard Goldstein also highlights the drama's central focus on family: "*An Early Frost* achieves its ambition, which is to fold the mythography of AIDS into the conflict between father and son … As the credits roll, the son has been reconciled with his family" (figure 9). Though "far from illiberal," the drama "is hardly empathetic or, for that matter, true to what people with AIDS have struggled to achieve" (Goldstein 1990, 307). Goldstein's comments on *An Early Frost* feature as part of a broader argument in which he draws a contrast between two different types of cultural texts that engage with HIV/AIDS. On the one hand are those which are nuanced and complex, centre on people with HIV and AIDS, and "implicate" us in the epidemic; and on the other hand are those which style themselves as "immune," and are "largely concerned with the society surrounding people with AIDS: the spouse, children, family, friends, and colleagues of the infected" (Goldstein 1990, 298).

Goldstein's critical perspective, which lambasts the mass media for its dissemination of "immune" texts, was articulated at the end of a decade of HIV/AIDS, years in which such cultural channels had often demonised seropositive people. As Harry Benshoff and Sean Griffin helpfully summarise, reflecting on the 1980s:

> Rather than treat people with AIDS as integrated human beings living with illness, the media focused on sensationalistic tropes of death, decay, victimization, and isolation. The media also tended to configure people with AIDS as either innocent (women and children who had gotten the disease inadvertently from blood transfusions) or deserving (intravenous drug users and sexually active gay men whose allegedly "aberrant lifestyles" had caused their illness). Mass media narratives about contagion, cure, plagues, and monsters were repeatedly invoked, as was a polarizing discourse about "us" (clean-living heterosexuals) versus "them" (disease-ridden queers). (Benshoff and Griffin 2006, 203)

This is what, elsewhere, Simon Watney refers to as "the *spectacle of AIDS*, constituted in a regime of massively overdetermined images, which are sensitive only to the values of the dominant familial 'truth' of AIDS" (Watney 1987, 78, italics original). Against such dominant discourses and forms of representation, it was politically vital for queer people to use film and video (and other

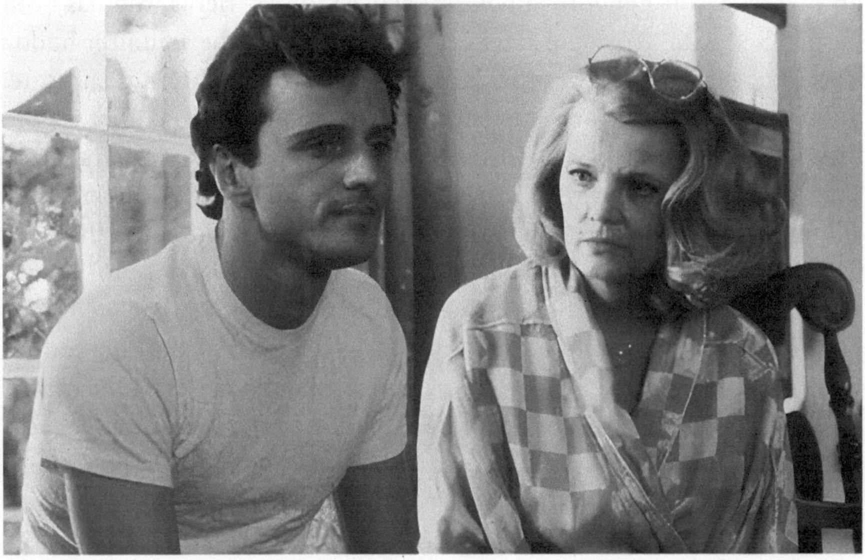

Figure 9
For some queer critics, *An Early Frost* (1985) was more concerned with the impact of AIDS on the family than with the experiences of people with AIDS – more "immune" than "implicated."

media) to craft their own stories, air their own voices, advance their own perspectives, and fight back against the pernicious and dangerous messages embedded in mainstream texts.

Two key films about HIV/AIDS of the mid-1980s were made independently and attempted to portray seropositive gay men in fresh and sympathetic ways. *Buddies* (1985) was written and directed by Arthur Bressan, who had previously made documentaries about gay life (such as *Gay USA*, 1977) and erotic/pornographic features (including *Forbidden Letters*, 1979). *Buddies* was shot in nine days on a budget of under $30,000 and distributed by independent New Line Cinema (whose subsidiary, Fine Line, would go on to distribute the key New Queer Cinema title *My Own Private Idaho* in 1991). *Buddies* focuses on Robert (Geoff Edholm), a political activist for gay rights who has been hospitalised with AIDS, and David (David Schachter), the volunteer buddy who has been assigned to provide Robert with companionship and care. Though the two men have different worldviews and initially do not get on, they come to forge a strong bond. Robert eventually dies while David, affected by their relationship, is moved to take part in activism. The film, Russo writes, "illuminates the emotional intensity of present-day gay life better than any disease-of-the-week, made-for-television drama could ever hope to" (Russo 1987, 274). It proved to be Bressan's last film, as he died of AIDS-related complications in 1987. *Parting Glances* (1986) was Bill Sherwood's only feature film.[3] Made for under $300,000 (a low budget, though ten times the cost of *Buddies*), the film's narrative takes place in one 24-hour period and focuses on a gay couple in New York, Robert (John Bolger) and Michael (Richard Ganoung). Robert is just about to leave town (and the country) for a new job, while Michael spends time caring for his friend and ex-partner, HIV-positive Nick (Steve Buscemi). (There is a noteworthy link between *Parting Glances* and New Queer Cinema: Sherwood's assistant editor on the film was Christine Vachon.) Both *Buddies* and *Parting Glances* offer important independent ripostes to mainstream "immune" depictions of HIV/AIDS. *Buddies* not only focuses on a community support system (a buddying volunteer service) that operates outside of and supplements mainstream health care, but explicitly connects encounters with the retrovirus to activism. Nick in *Parting Glances*, meanwhile, as Thomas Yingling notes, "is defined by excess rather than absence" and "refuses repentance as the appropriate response to his AIDS diagnosis" (Yingling 1997, 28). Further, as Thomas Waugh highlights, both films depict HIV-positive men as sexual agents, a representational strategy that "constitutes a defiant articulation of desire and sexual identity in the face of the stereotypes, the taboos, and the death we know so well" (Waugh 2000, 223).

Waugh also points out that many of the initial responses to HIV/AIDS in independent film and video took the form of melodramas. Discussing titles made between 1984 and 1986 including *Buddies* and *Parting Glances*, he notes that the genre "was the principal vehicle ... for our dealing culturally with the trauma, fear, bereavement, and sacrifice that AIDS has occasioned in our community" (Waugh 2000, 219). He further suggests that these melodramatic works serve in retrospect as a prophetic preview of a subsequent surge in melodramatic queer films about HIV/AIDS which included quasi-independent fare such as *Longtime Companion* (1989), mainstream titles like *Philadelphia* (1993), and more experimental work such as John Greyson's *Zero Patience* (1993), a film usually seen as part of the New Queer Cinema corpus. (Elsewhere, Waugh identifies Laurie Lynd's short film *RSVP*, discussed in the previous chapter, as another key text in the 1990s swell of queer melodramas [Waugh 2006, 280].)

Longtime Companion was funded by American Playhouse, the PBS programming strand, with a budget of around $1.5 million. Distributed by the independent company Samuel Goldwyn, it went on to gross $4.6 million at the box office. The film's narrative follows, across the span of the 1980s, the impact of HIV and AIDS on a group of relatively affluent white gay friends and lovers. Progressively, the group diminishes in size as individuals succumb to the disease. Towards the close of the decade, those remaining become involved in community politics: answering helpline calls at Gay Men's Health Crisis, organising money-raising benefits, taking part in a buddy programme, attending ACT UP demonstrations. *Longtime Companion* ends with three characters walking on a beach, where in a brief shared fantasy sequence they are joined by all of those they have lost to AIDS (figure 10). As with *An Early Frost*, some queer writers criticise the film for being toothless: "The style of *Longtime Companion*," writes Roy Grundmann, "seems to grow out of the urge to communicate to the mainstream audience the problems caused by AIDS that gays have known about and learned to live with for a long time." Because the characters only represent a narrow and privileged sector of society, "their fates must ring hollow to those who as yet have no access to the expensive AZT, to hospital beds, or psychological support" (Grundmann 1990, 48). Other critics are more generous. Watney, for instance, sees the film as "implicated" rather

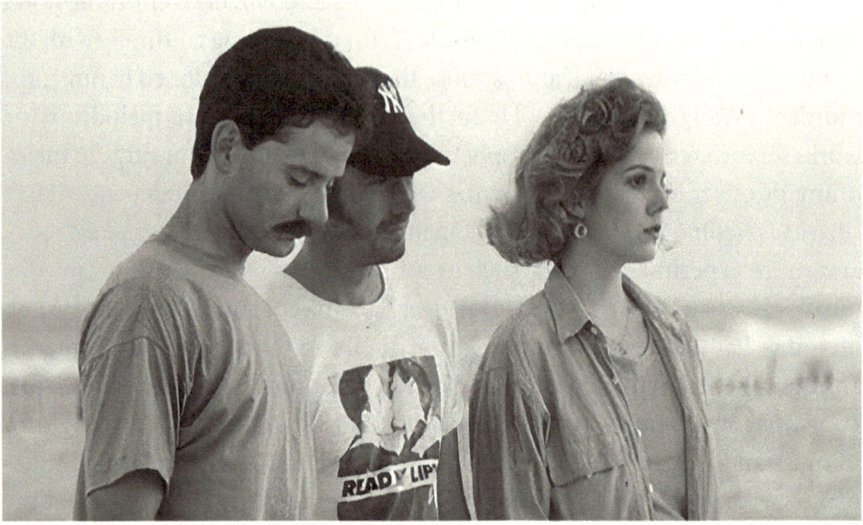

Figure 10
Willy (Campbell Scott), Fuzzy (Stephen Caffrey), and Lisa (Mary-Louise Parker) together face an uncertain future at the end of *Longtime Companion* (1989).

than "immune" (to invoke Goldstein's dichotomy), and writes that it "helps non-Americans to begin, at least, to understand the nightmare of the American epidemic, and for the first time, allows straight Americans to think about gay men as people in many respects like themselves. This is no mean achievement" (Watney 1992, 165).[4]

In addition to the small smattering of feature-length films made in the 1980s that depict the impact of HIV and AIDS on queer characters, their friends, and their families, artists and activists also used film and video in more experimental ways to engage with the pandemic. Several directors who would go on to be associated with New Queer Cinema produced works directly concerned with HIV/AIDS: Tom Kalin, Isaac Julien, John Greyson. Kalin first used video to confront AIDS in the mid-1980s as a student at the Art Institute of Chicago, with his works *Like Little Soldiers* and *News from Home* (the latter made with Stathis Lagoudikis) exploring personal fears about infection and disclosing one's seropositivity. *they are lost to vision altogether* (1988) is a thirteen-minute speedy collage of materials (photographs, television, and film extracts) with original footage. The director refers to it as an act of "erotic retaliation" against legislation such as the Helms Amendment, "an attempt to reclaim eroticism and to address the contradictions of sexuality and romance in the face of a monolithic and culturally compulsory heterosexuality."[5] In an overview of his early film and video career, Alexandra Juhasz writes that Kalin "makes tapes for ghosts: the people he has lost to AIDS, the faces he has seen on city streets or at AIDS demonstrations. He says that 'they mark the terrifying feeling of being a person among many people. They are a lullaby I sing to myself to reassure myself and they are also a cry for help'" (Juhasz 1995, 60).

Both Julien and Greyson, working in different national contexts, made short videos that counteracted dominant media messaging about HIV transmission, safer sex, and the potential threat of the pandemic. Julien's *This Is Not an AIDS Advertisement* (1988), produced under the umbrella of the Sankofa Film and Video Workshop, is in two parts. In the first, romantic piano music plays over looped and layered images: an embracing interracial male pair offering a bouquet of flowers to the camera; solo portrait shots of each; dappled sunlight on water; light through an arched window; a tree canopy; gravestones; water traversed at speed in a boat. In the second, a funky dance-oriented pop track plays over imagery repeated from the first part (the couple with flowers, sunlight on water, and so on), with the addition of new footage of posed models, solo and in pairs, reminiscent of fashion magazine shoots. A male voice says, "This is not an AIDS advertisement – feel no guilt in your desire," the words appearing on screen in tandem with his speech. Throughout both halves, imagery is manipulated with filters, and its tempo is altered. Created the year after the UK government paid millions of pounds to create its sinister "Monolith" and "Iceberg" AIDS prevention campaign adverts,

Julien's ten-minute video used alternative registers (romantic, upbeat pop) to propose hopeful visions of pandemic-era queer life. In a similar vein, in Greyson's five-minute cheerful musical *The* ADS *Epidemic* (1989), which draws some of its characters from Thomas Mann's classic of unrequited queer lust *Death in Venice*, Aschenbach falls prey to ADS ("acquired dread of sex") and his object of desire Tadzio learns about safer sex.

By the turn of the 1990s, then, the directors of the films that came to be known as New Queer Cinema were able to produce their work against a background of several years'-worth of HIV/AIDS-related film and video: queer attempts to use the moving image to engage with the realities and felt experience of life with HIV and AIDS. These attempts primarily took the form of melodramatic feature narratives or experimental artistic short videos – distinct formats with very different modes of address and relationships to story. After a decade of AIDS-related deaths, though, as Rich states, a political impasse caused by despair, anger, and frustration had been reached: what more could be done with the moving image to account for and reckon with the tragedy that continued to unfold on a daily basis?

New Queer Cinema and HIV/AIDS

As I noted in the opening pages of this chapter, José Arroyo argues that "AIDS is why there is New Queer Cinema and it is what New Queer Cinema is about." In comparison with the small volume of films and videos about HIV/AIDS, narrative and experimental, produced in the previous years, a fresh, dynamic, urgent, and angry form of activist practice now emerged. In his 1993 essay, Arroyo provides sustained analyses of *My Own Private Idaho* and *Edward II*, which he identifies as engaging with the epidemic in distinct ways. The former, he notes, "is not about AIDS in a conventional sense," with HIV/AIDS not mentioned by its characters; however, he proposes the epidemic as "*Idaho*'s absent cause and an important interpretative context" (Arroyo 1993, 72). Mike

Scott, the hustler played by River Phoenix, is a narcoleptic whose health suffers throughout the film: he is often shown cold, sniffling, bracing himself against the elements. As Arroyo writes, "It is easy to read Mike's narcolepsy as a displacement of AIDS. Mike's shivering, his lack of energy, his pallor, and his thinness contribute to the symptomatology" (Arroyo 1993, 79). Beyond this, Phoenix's character moves in a world of risk: of unpredictable sexual encounters with johns, of scruffy and illegitimate places to spend the night, of hardscrabble attempts to source enough money to eat. His challenging living circumstances, that is to say, make him susceptible to HIV.

Edward II is aesthetically a very different film to *Idaho*: Derek Jarman filmed his adaptation of Christopher Marlowe's play on a spartan theatrical set with minimal but extravagant props and costumes, deploying exaggerated characters and performances (figure 11). As Arroyo articulates, the film also operates with a different understanding of identity: *Edward II* is more evidently informed by the politics of gay liberation than the queerly inflected malleable conceptions of sexuality showcased in *Idaho*. (Although Edward's army is depicted at one point as placard-carrying protestors from OutRage, a British queer activist group, Jarman's film is underpinned by an essentialist and binary understanding of sexual orientation.) And yet, Arroyo argues, both *Idaho* and *Edward II* share some key characteristics: flamboyant stylistic eruptions, yearning romanticism, a disruptive use of time and chronology, and a dystopian outlook. *Idaho* ends with Mike back on the road, facing an uncertain future and relying on others' benevolence. Marlowe's play concludes with Edward being killed with a red-hot poker; Jarman's film ends more ambivalently, but with a markedly mournful tone. Indeed, Arroyo suggests that the films that make up New Queer Cinema can more broadly be "read as works of mourning." This mourning, he suggests, following Douglas Crimp, can be drawn on as an affective spur to militancy. As he concludes, films such as *Idaho* and *Edward II* "are not only attempts to represent a new historical context for gay men. Their very existence constitutes an effort to change it" (Arroyo 1993, 94).

Monica Pearl develops Arroyo's ideas about New Queer Cinema and HIV/AIDS further in an essay on Jarman's autobiographical *Blue* (1993) – a feature-length experimental film in which a collage of voices, music, and sounds accompany a static, blue image plane that does not alter. Although many New Queer Cinema films are not overtly about AIDS, she writes, the movement "is a form and expression that emerges from the cataclysm of AIDS in the Western world." Pearl highlights that HIV is a retrovirus which "does not follow the 'traditional' trajectory of infection" and argues that "the lack of coherent narrative, or genre recognition, or familiarly fulfilled cinematic expectations in New Queer Cinema, is partly a representational, or 'artistic,' reaction to the nature of retroviral behaviour. In other words, representation mimics the 'narrative' of the virus" (Pearl 2004, 24). Thus, she claims, *Blue* is a New Queer Cinema film because it is "formally 'fragmented' and challenging," and because it "disrupts visual and narrative expectations" (Pearl 2004, 28, 29). New Queer Cinema, she concludes, is less concerned with telling a coherent story than with depicting life with the virus in an authentic manner. The movement, she writes, "provides another way of making sense out of the virus, that does not placate and does not provide easy answers" (Pearl 2004, 33).

Here, we can return to Todd Haynes's *Poison* and Laurie Lynd's *RSVP*, both of which I briefly discussed in chapter 1 in relation to Rich's characterisation of "Homo Pomo" and neither of which are examined by Arroyo or Pearl. *Poison* is not explicitly about HIV/AIDS, but the epidemic again operates as a vital context for making sense of the film. In line with Pearl's arguments, we can now see the film's fractured structure as an instance of retroviral narrative form. Although the sci-fi/horror pastiche strand of *Poison* seems to most evidently be concerned with infection and bodily decline, other aspects of the film more subtly suggest HIV and AIDS. *Poison* largely adopts a downbeat or dystopian perspective: an intertitle states that "the whole world is dying of panicky fright." Both the "Horror" narrative and the "Hero" fake documentary strand carry echoes of a "patient zero" narrative. As Justin Wyatt writes, Doctor

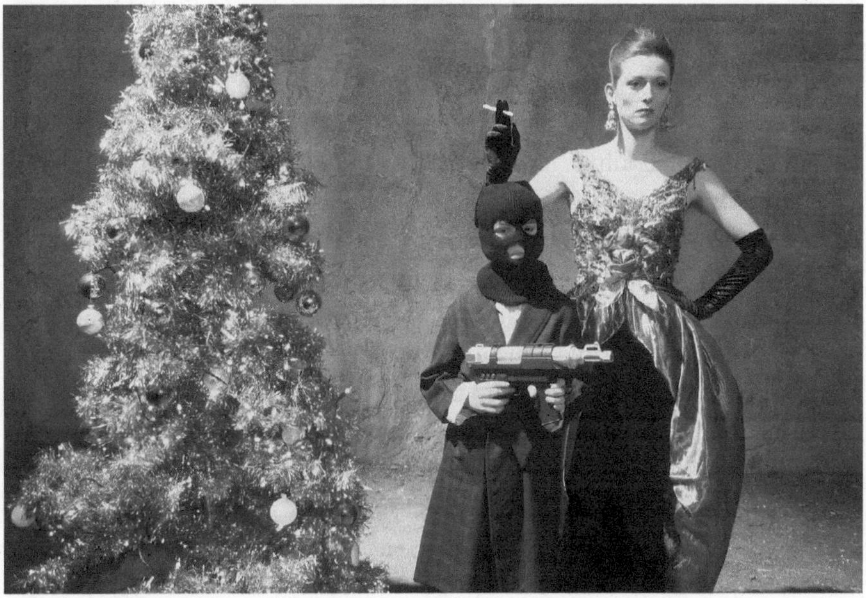

Figure 11
The extravagant props and outfits of Derek Jarman's *Edward II* (1991) contrast with its spartan set.

Graves (the central protagonist in the horror pastiche) is an "unwitting starting point for the contagion," and Richie (the missing child who is the focus of the fake documentary) is positioned as a "target for widespread public attack" (Wyatt 1998, 33) – indeed, the attribution of blame is a primary concern in *Poison*. For Wyatt, Haynes's film also draws lessons from Gran Fury and its activist deployment of mainstream media and aesthetics, such as advertising, to deliver challenging and disruptive messages: "Haynes' invocation of pop culture media forms and structures, as well as the larger institutional structure of the art cinema, allows him to present a kind of social activism and protest to specific and targeted audiences" (Wyatt 1998, 34). Haynes's film can be seen, then, as one attempt to comprehend the virus, including individual, community, and political responses to it.

RSVP, I suggested in the previous chapter, uses simple and unshowy means to convey its elegiac narrative; I've also noted its affiliation with a wave of melodramatic queer films. And yet the short film does not straightforwardly tell a conventional tale of mourning, of familial discord and reparation. As Ross Chambers identifies, Lynd's film operates through a layering of deferrals and mediations which interrupt linear time: the radio programme *RSVP* only processes Andrew's request to hear Jessye Norman after his death; answerphone messages are missed (purposefully or not); Sid is a photographer, his images commuting moments from the past to the present viewer; the broadcast reaches different audiences in distinct time zones at different times; and so on. This extends to the lyrics of Norman's aria, narrated by a rose from a realm beyond to the woman who wore it to a ball: "This faint perfume is my soul, and I come to you from paradise." Through these layers, Chambers argues, *RSVP* identifies "deferral as a price of survival" (Chambers 1997, 71). The film also includes sequences which venture into abstraction. As Andrew's parents listen to the aria on the radio, for instance, we see various disconnected images: a suburban street; children playing in a yard; a deforested area of land; a school bus static on a country lane, lights flashing; a muddy field with a busy road in the distance; high rise buildings; and so on. This might be the geographical expanse across which CBC is broadcasting, radio waves permeating the nation; more allegorically, the sequence could indicate the reach of HIV/AIDS and its impact on diverse communities.

The Living End is both overtly about HIV/AIDS and, in form and composition, an attempt to convey and reveal its broader impact on queer communities. In what remains of this chapter, I first unpack the film's explicit engagement with HIV/AIDS and how this differs from or challenges dominant representational tactics, and second look at more subtle and complex ways in which it can be comprehended as "an AIDS movie." Jon's diagnosis comes very early in the film, at around the two-minute mark. The doctor's droll, disaffected delivery of the verdict demonstrates a lack of compassion (even though his camp tone and office décor hint that he himself is gay): the suggestion is that the medical establishment does not care about yet another gay man infected with HIV. Jon reacts with physical shock, vomiting into a toilet, while the doctor (in voiceover) delivers advice about "safe sex" practices appropriate to "high risk" demographics, articulating the mainstream rhetoric and understanding of how the virus needs to be managed. The Dictaphone journal entry that frames Jon's visit to the doctor seems to draw an affective equivalence between shopping for a CD and getting the results of his HIV test, but the shot of him vomiting reveals the emotional punch he has received.

Jon visits Darcy at her apartment to tell her about his diagnosis. Before and after this scene, Araki inserts two short snippets of hazy news footage, complete with visual interference bars. The first consists of three short shots: of officials in white shirts attending to bodies lying on the ground; of a sole official kneeling next to a figure covered in blood; of a solitary corpse (figure 12). A male voiceover delivers the words "another death, another brutal killing."[6] The sequence of the three images progressively removes authority figures from the frame, the victims of atrocity initially tended to but then abandoned. The second, shorter clip has just one shot, of a number of bodies lined up together on the ground. These two brief extracts seem to be of footage from a war zone. It is feasible that these scenes are playing on a television in Darcy's apartment: as she and Jon talk, there is incoherent chatter in the background, and there are no hard audio cuts between the clips and the pair's conversation. Alternatively, they may represent Jon's state of mind so soon after his diagnosis, articulating a vision of HIV/AIDS as a rampaging force annihilating communities. Either way, the inclusion and positioning of these scenes intervenes in the narrative to draw an explicit association between AIDS and other forms of global carnage. The news footage serves as the only irruption of "the real" in *The Living End*, a strategic utilisation of documentary material to analogously articulate the effect of HIV and AIDS on gay men. And yet, Araki's use of these clips is also open to critique: drawing a brisk parallel between an unspecified war zone and an infectious epidemic erases the distinctions between these different, terrible (and differently terrible) circumstances.

We do not witness Jon coming out to Darcy as HIV positive. That moment has already passed: as we join their conversation, Darcy moves to querying whether Jon was "careful," and the pair jointly suspect that the source of Jon's infection was his ex, Craig, who has now moved back in with his parents in Utah (suggesting, perhaps, that he is very sick). Soon after, when Jon has brought Luke home and the hustler seduces him, Jon stalls the foreplay. He is about to disclose his HIV-positive status but Luke stops him: "If you're trying to say what I think you are, don't worry about it. It's really no big deal. Welcome to the club, partner." *The Living End* refuses to furnish its audiences with the standard "coming out as positive" scene which many fictional dramas about HIV/AIDS include – one which, of course, adds a second layer of queer "confession" to the standard "coming out as gay" sequence. Jon later owns his seropositive status: soon after he and Luke hit the road for San Francisco, he grumbles that "forty-eight hours ago, I was just another bummed-out, HIV-positive homo minding my own business. Now I'm a fugitive." Luke dismisses Jon's self-pity (and his slippery relationship to labels and identities) with a phatic response: "Yeah, well, the world is a big, confusing place, isn't it?"

Luke's suggestion that those infected with HIV are members of a "club" accentuates the "positivity" in "seropositivity." Indeed, the morning after Jon and Luke first have sex, Luke voices his liberatory understanding of life with the virus. He acknowledges that he and Jon are going to die, "maybe in ten years, maybe next week," arguing that HIV "is all part of the Neo-Nazi Republican Final Solution," and describing the retrovirus as "germ warfare" and "genocide."[7] Jon accuses him of being paranoid. Luke proceeds, however, to articulate a radical queer politics of alterity: "There's thousands, maybe millions of us walking around with this thing inside of us, this time-bomb ticking, you know, making our futures finite. Suddenly I realise: we've got nothing to lose. We can say fuck work. Fuck the system. Fuck everything. Don't you get

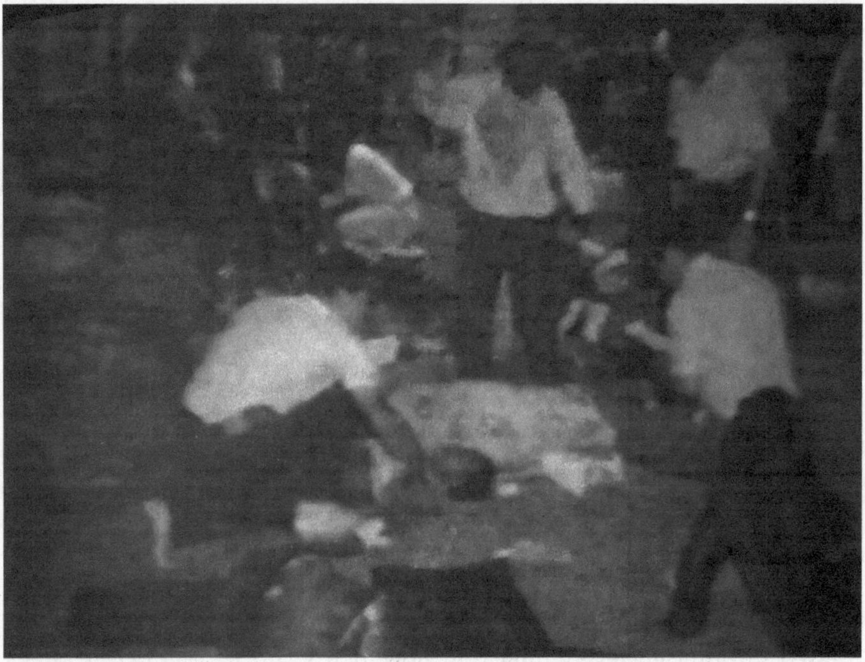

Figure 12
A brief interruption of news footage in *The Living End* draws a connection between HIV/AIDS and other forms of global humanitarian disaster.

it? We're totally free. We can do whatever the fuck we want to do." Being HIV positive, reasons Luke, positions the pair (and everyone else living with the virus) outside of heteronormative society and its moral and legal codes. Facing impending and inevitable death, employment and the wider world of regulations and good behaviour it represents become meaningless. Above Jon and Luke's heads, a child on a Smiths poster winces while sucking on an ice lolly: Luke's thesis may be chilling, but it's also delicious. The next scene demonstrates Luke's philosophy: he and Jon go on a spree with a purloined credit card. As they banter on the street, carrying their new purchases, a blond neo-Nazi provokes them with homophobic threats and slurs. Out of frame, Luke beats him up with a boombox. This is a step too far for Jon, who kicks Luke out of his apartment. What is notable here (and, indeed, in the earlier shooting of the "three stooges") is that Luke's violent actions rhyme, in exaggerated form, with those advocated by political groups such as Queer Nation whose 1990 manifesto ("Queers Read This") exhorts queer people to "bash back": "Let yourself be angry that the price of our visibility is the constant threat of violence, anti-queer violence to which practically every segment of this society contributes" (see Howell 2015, 123).

Jon and Luke's seropositivity positions them as rebels, abandoned and rejected by the mainstream, and thus architects of their own codes of living. Jon quite quickly accepts Luke back, joining him on the lam after Luke (seemingly) kills a cop. At one point on the road, Luke advocates heading to Washington and blowing President Bush's brains out – or "better yet, we can hold him at gunpoint and inject him with a syringeful of our blood. How much do you want to bet they'd have a Magic Cure by tomorrow?" Jon is not impressed, sardonically responding, "Oh, now there's a great idea"; in fact, Luke's extreme perspective never fully wins him over. And yet Luke's suggestions are not too far from the kinds of radical interventions that some queer activist groups such as ACT UP formulated and carried out. Of course, such groups never advocated murder, but Luke's proposals register the anger and frustration felt by so many of their members.

Dramatic fictions such as *Buddies* and *Longtime Companion* deploy melodrama and "illness of the week" elements to build sympathetic HIV-positive characters who grow ever more frail, their susceptibility to illness revealing their common humanity. Neither Luke nor Jon have this character arc. Indeed, neither exhibit any of the common conditions used to mark the typical mediated "AIDS victim": Kaposi's sarcoma lesions, ashen complexion, sores around the mouth, a physical wasting. Scenes of Luke pissing (outside a gated garden, up a sandy scree) and shitting might be read as subtle intimations of issues with his health – though, equally, they could just indicate the quantity of Jack Daniel's he drinks and fast food he consumes. Indeed, throughout *The Living End*, Luke remains a buff and tanned icon of muscular fitness (during the shoot, while the rest of the cast munched on chop suey, Mike Dytri ate cans of tuna to keep himself in shape). The film's only clear depiction of physical weakness is later, when Jon becomes unwell. His sweating, coughing, and tiredness could (like Mike's sniffling in *My Own Private Idaho*) be read as an analogy for AIDS-related infection. Equally, it could be nothing more than a common cold. Crucially, as Kylo-Patrick Hart notes, *The Living End* does not conform to "the expected ending of many movies pertaining to HIV/AIDS, especially those that were made and released during the pandemic's first decade": neither of the protagonists die (Hart 2010, 22). Araki does not allow such a payoff, stranding Jon and Luke in infected limbo.

Beyond all of these literal engagements with HIV/AIDS, it is also worth examining how *The Living End* is a product more broadly of the epidemic. As Pearl writes of the film, "What makes it New Queer Cinema is not the ways that it is overtly about AIDS, but the ways that it is preoccupied with death and time and history" (Pearl 2004, 28). In addition to the killings Luke perpetrates, or that occur in close proximity to him, signs and symbols of death proliferate widely across *The Living End*. Jon's car has a sticker on the boot that reads "Choose Death," which is both a witty riposte to the popular 1980s "Choose Life" T-shirts designed by Katharine Hamnett, and also a stark contrast to the "Silence = Death" emblem that became a defining graphic of late 1980s queer activism. Skulls appear on the doctor's desk, on the bandana worn by one of the lesbian killers, in a kitschy globe light next to Jon's telephone (figure 13), on an earring Luke wears; skeletons dangle from Darcy's earlobes and on the inside of Jon's closet door (figure 14). Jon and Luke, on the road, discuss the suicide of Joy Division singer Ian Curtis, the afterlife, and Luke's desire to kill himself at the first sign of a symptom of AIDS. Luke also regales Jon with an anecdote about witnessing a homeless woman commit suicide by jumping off a skyscraper ("landed feet first, bounced back up like ten feet in the air"). But most significantly, the prospect of an early death underpins Luke's rebellious philosophy, his dissident politics. As Pearl puts it, "This film boldly suggests that for those marginalised by the world – by sexual identity, but not only by that – the spectre of death makes one more empowered, more free, than one was before one was haunted by that spectre" (Pearl 2004, 28).

Pearl, as noted above, argues that New Queer Cinema shares qualities with HIV: it tends to lack a coherent narrative and fails to satisfy familiar and generic expectations. Unlike some instances of the movement, such as *Poison* or *My Own Private Idaho*, the structure of *The Living End* is almost entirely

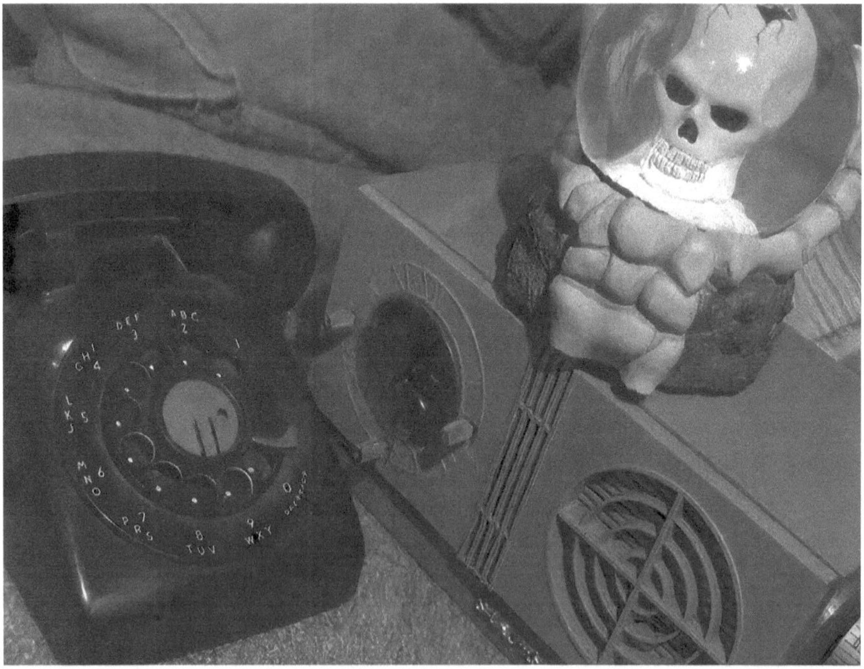

Figures 13 and 14
Signifiers of death abound in *The Living End*'s mise-en-scène including, in Jon's apartment, a skull globe light and a skeleton in the closet.

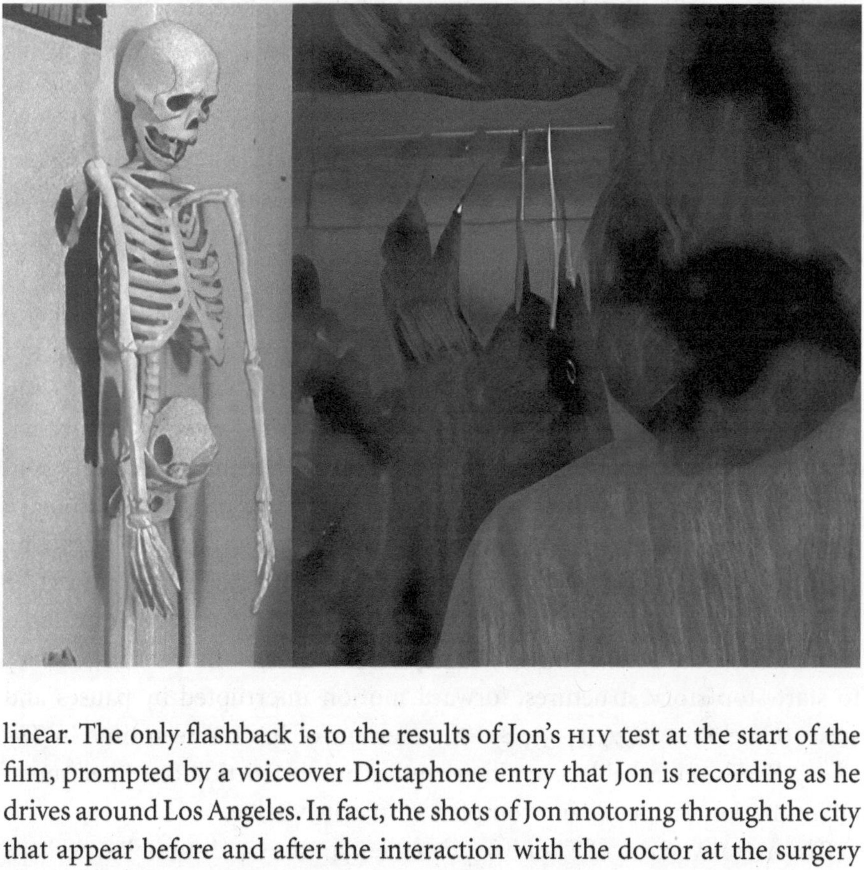

linear. The only flashback is to the results of Jon's HIV test at the start of the film, prompted by a voiceover Dictaphone entry that Jon is recording as he drives around Los Angeles. In fact, the shots of Jon motoring through the city that appear before and after the interaction with the doctor at the surgery may also be flashbacks: in them, Jon is behind the wheel, seemingly preoccupied, and not using his Dictaphone. The machine only appears around three minutes into the film, after Jon drives past a shirtless, hitchhiking Luke and does not slow down for him; from this moment on, the narrative unfurls chronologically. It is as though the positive test result both effects a rupture in time and also partly disconnects the chronological alignment of the film's audio and visual channels; it is only Jon and Luke's first glancing proximity that sets the plot on a linear course.

What is notable about the structure of *The Living End*, however, is that it stutters. Brief sections of black screen repeatedly interrupt the flow of the narrative, inserting beats between many (though not all) scenes. None are silent, full interruptions: audio continues from the previous shot, or begins playing for the shot to follow, but the visual channel is blocked. During one section on the road, as the pair discuss Ian Curtis's death and Luke expresses his desire to die "with a big bang and a big fucking smile on my face," each shot is separated from the next by a short black break; the audio channel of Jon and Luke's conversation is continuous. This interruptive aesthetic device is not one that Araki uses in his first two films, *Three Bewildered People* and *The Long Weekend*, though those stutter in their own ways: as Daryl Chin writes of these earlier works, "the rhythms that Araki establishes through editing are often choppy, emphasizing discord rather than continuity, and eliciting discomfort" (Chin 1993, 106–7). The effect of the beats is to make the structure of *The Living End* episodic, with the interruptions signifying an unspecified amount of time passing. This fragmented format might be explained in part by the film's generic debt to the road movie (a topic explored in more detail in the next chapter): Corey Creekmur notes the genre's tendency to start-stop story structures, forward motion interrupted by pauses and stasis (Creekmur 1997, 94–5). But the amount of black screen time in *The Living End* is remarkable, each interruption an obstruction or impediment, an intimation that a full and complete stop is inevitable.

The narrative form of *The Living End* then, sputters and stumbles, perhaps affected by the retrovirus. But there are other viral manifestations in the film: most notably, as Roy Grundmann notes, "Luke infects Jon like a virus, and we are infected along with him"; indeed, "infection blurs with infatuation" (Grundmann 1993, 27). Araki's film opens with Luke, and he has his own narrative adventures (with Daisy and Fern, with Ken and Barbie, with the three stooges) before his story intersects with Jon's. But an argument could be made that he is a personification of HIV, unpredictable and dangerous, and that he exists solely as a figment of Jon's imagination. Darcy never meets Luke: she just hears about him. For the recently diagnosed Jon, a hunky and fit porn-stereotype drifter would seem unattainable, a remote and idealised figure about whom to safely fantasise. (The film takes for granted that there is a mutual attraction between Jon and Luke, but what is it in Jon that Luke finds appealing?) Over the arc of the film, Jon butts his head against Luke's philosophical understanding of the freedoms afforded by seropositivity, being simultaneously seduced and repelled by the implications. The film's conclusion serves as a savage physical and intellectual reckoning: forced to have anal sex in a public space, raped by the retrovirus incarnate, Jon realises that only uncertainty lies ahead.

Chapter 3

Style and Content

In the previous chapter, my sustained exploration of *The Living End* as a key instance of "retroviral cinema" began to articulate a close reading of the film's content and shape. In this chapter, I pick up this process of analysis and dissect *The Living End*'s generic form, its intertextual references and uses of pastiche and appropriation; its mise-en-scène (paying particular attention to locations, props, costume, and performance), and its soundtrack and music.

Genre

When B. Ruby Rich attended Toronto's Festival of Festivals in 1991, the queer films she saw seemed to be "annexing whole genres." The titles screened included *My Own Private Idaho*, which borrowed elements of the road movie and the Shakesperean history play for its narrative of two street hustlers from disparate backgrounds and the rift that grows between them; and *Edward II*, which reworked and embellished Marlowe's play with agitprop politics, anachronistic detail, and musical interludes, explicitly articulating Edward's relationship with his confidante Gaveston as a sexual one. As with these two films, the generic categorisation of *The Living End* is not straightforward, as it borrows and blends aspects of distinct forms.

The first thing that viewers of *The Living End* see on screen, in blue lettering on a black background, is "an irresponsible movie by gregg araki" (with no capital letters). This sets expectation and a tone: the intention to agitate, to provoke. However, the use of the word "irresponsible" is a nod to a very specific source. In his book on the director Howard Hawks, first published in 1968, Robin Wood argues that the adventure films made by Hawks, such as *Rio Bravo* (1959), "place high value on the sense of responsibility," while in contrast his comedies "derive much of their tension and intensity from the fascination exerted by irresponsibility" (Wood 1983, 68). A key example of the latter that Wood discusses is *Bringing Up Baby* (1938). In this screwball, sensible palaeontologist David Huxley (Cary Grant) is due to marry, but the day before his wedding he meets loose cannon Susan Vance (Katharine Hepburn). They swiftly become embroiled in a series of mishaps and adventures, largely centred on a tame leopard called Baby. Despite their distinctly different characters, the two fall in love, and David resigns himself to the bedlam and turmoil of spending his life with Susan (figure 15). Hepburn's character, writes Wood, "shatters to fragments the superficial order" of David's life. "Once she has materialised, he is completely helpless against her ... She is not so much *im*moral as *a*moral: she seems never to feel a twinge of guilt, never acknowledging responsibility for the comic disasters she precipitates" (Wood 1983, 70, italics original). The narrative of the film progresses, argues Wood, "from the world of the dominance of the Superego to that of the Id," and "from the unnatural order of the museum to the natural disorder of the woods at night" (Wood 1983, 70, 71). Viewers are left questioning "whether the triumph of total irresponsibility the film appears to be offering as fitting resolution is in fact acceptable" (Wood 1983, 71).

In a number of interviews, Araki identifies both Hawks's film and Wood's writing on it as influential. The structure of Hawks's film, he says, "is kind of the same as *The Living End* in that it was about this spirited, free-willed character who frees this repressed, more normal-life character. So *The Living End*

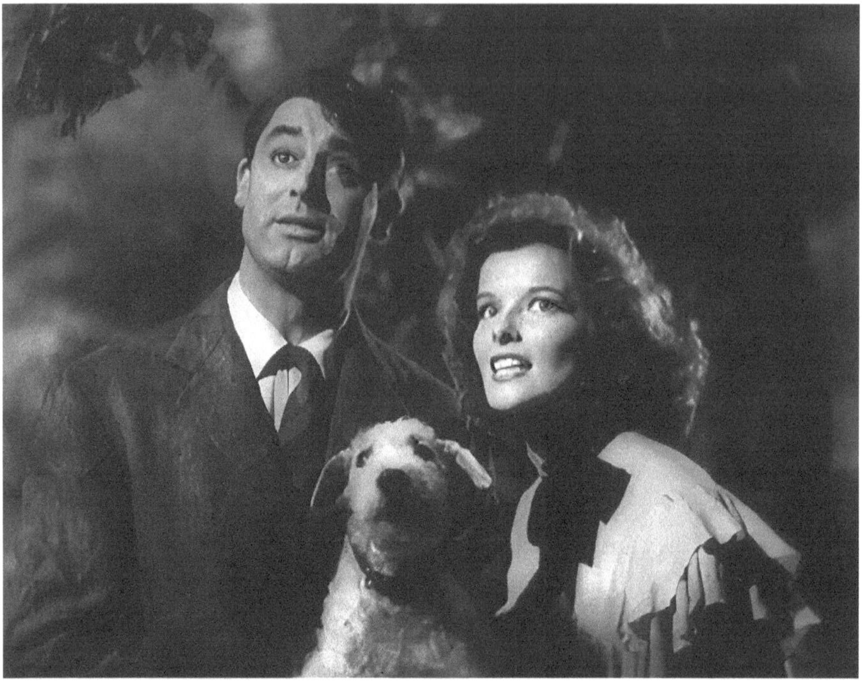

Figure 15
A key inspiration behind *The Living End* was *Bringing Up Baby* (1938) – and Robin Wood's writing on the film, which discusses "the lure of irresponsibility."

sort of fit that paradigm. Also, the whole film has a very irreverent and anarchic point of view" (Smith 2008). This avowed connection invites reflection on the extent to which *The Living End* is a screwball comedy. Consider Dana Polan's outline of the main forms taken by the genre:

> In one typical variant of screwball, a couple is split up (whether by external causes or by internalised doubts about the marriage) and, knowing intuitively but correctly that the love hasn't really gone out of the

> relationship, the abandoned party plots and connives to get his/her lover back … In a second variant, an energetic and even outrageous person recognises in a member of the opposite sex kindred qualities that are being crushed by bourgeois respectability and schemes to win the kindred soul away from respectability into a world of madcap adventure. (Polan 1993, 16)

In both variants, argues Polan, characters have to deploy tricks and tactics to seduce each other. These films tend to take place in urban locations – "the city as the site where innocence has been lost" – but, through plot developments, characters will leave the city and end up in more natural environments, where they "can discover or rediscover the love they seemed to have lost under the pressures of city life" (Polan 1993, 16, 17).

Although there are substantive differences between *Bringing Up Baby* and *The Living End*, it is possible to apply Wood and Polan's writings fairly neatly to Araki's film. The narrative of *The Living End* can be seen to enact the second screwball variant Polan outlines: Luke is "energetic and even outrageous," and he liberates Jon from "bourgeois respectability." Although Jon occasionally attempts to reassert an earlier status quo, to revive or sustain aspects of his former existence, he is seduced by the alternative and exciting world Luke represents. As emblematic of this shift, Jon's pet goldfish Craig, named after his ex, dies while he is on the road with Luke. Although Jon remembers to ask Darcy to feed the fish, his prompt comes too late: she discovers the corpse on the floor of his flat (suggesting it leapt, suicidally, from the bowl). Similarly, when Jon attempts at one motel to resume recording his Dictaphone entries, the batteries turn out to be dead, and Luke dismisses the idea of the journal as "bogus." Following Wood's formulation, Luke is an amoral figure who never expresses a "twinge of guilt": he justifies his catalogue of bad behaviours via a philosophy of sexual alterity that puts him outside of the mainstream, "totally free." Indeed, Luke can be seen to represent the force of the id to Jon's superego: he is a lusty, booze-swigging, violence-prone figure, whose romantic impulses are also excessive ("I love you more than life," he tells Jon). The couple's road trip ends on a beach, a space of "natural disorder," beyond the sprawl and urban clamour of any metropolis: the only sounds over the film's final credits are waves and the wind.

Can we see particular aspects of *The Living End* as a riff on, or riposte to, facets of *Bringing Up Baby*? Might we see Hepburn's spectacular gowns in *Bringing Up Baby* (designed by Howard Greer) as substituted, in *The Living End*, by Luke-as-spectacle, his leather jacket, shades, and ripped jeans establishing him as object of contemplation? While such comparisons, however speculative or forced, are fun to entertain, Araki's main borrowing from Hawks's film is evidently a structural one, the forces of irresponsibility crashing into (and largely winning out over) responsibility. To this, he adds other generic elements: most obviously, the road movie. Indeed, in the press kit for *The Living End*, Araki does not mention Hawks, instead describing the film as a "Couple on the Run movie in the tradition of Lang's *You Only Live Once*, Ray's *They Live by Night*, Godard's *Pierrot le Fou* and Malick's *Badlands*" (Araki 1992). In a scene that appears in the screenplay but not the film, the characters explicitly and self-reflexively name generic landmarks:

> Luke: Hey, y'know, this is sorta like that movie …
> Jon: What? *They Live by Night*? *Gun Crazy*? *Pierrot le Fou*? *Badlands*?
> Luke: No, the one with Richard Gere and that French chick. (Araki 1994, 41)[1]

Beyond these particular reference points, and expanding the scope of his road movie pantheon to include comedy, Araki also describes the film as "like a Hope/Crosby movie … in which Crosby fucks Hope" (Anon 1992, 60). Reviews from the time of its release often compare *The Living End* to Ridley Scott's feminist road movie *Thelma and Louise* (1991): Stephen Holden in *The New York Times*, for instance, described Araki's film as "a gay, post-punk *Thelma and Louise*" (Holden 1992, C20). But Scott's film appeared in cinemas after *The Living End* had been written and shot – and Araki wasn't too impressed with it. "I didn't much like *Thelma and Louise*," he told Matthew Hays; "I thought it was too preachy and heavy-handed" (Hays 2007, 39).

Both *Thelma and Louise* and *The Living End* contributed to an early 1990s resurgence of the road movie in mainstream and independent US cinema. Until the 1990s, queer characters were notably lacking from the genre: indeed, perhaps the only instance in which gay male characters briefly and overtly appear is *Vanishing Point* (1971). This absence is, most likely, connected to the association of the genre with heterosexual masculinity: as Marita Sturken notes, the "classic road movie was about male privilege, the right to hit the road without worrying about the kids or a destination" (Sturken 2000, 39). Many of the films in the early 1990s road movie boom, however, feature marginalized protagonists (women, Native Americans and other people of colour, disabled people) and subject the genre's structure, themes, and iconography to interrogation. What did it mean to admit the previously excluded to centre stage (or rather, to the driver's seat) in these films? Could the generic template be subverted, reclaimed, worked over, and what was the relationship of the marginalized or subaltern protagonists to the landscape through which they travelled? As Michael Atkinson asks, rhetorically, "Why make a '90s road movie if not to transgress the genre's timeworn iconography?" (Atkinson 1994, 14).

Despite the straight, masculine affiliations that there may be with the genre, the road movie also carries associations with the outsider, the renegade, the dissenter, who pushes back against constricting societal limits on behaviour. As Katie Mills notes, the genre thus "offers marginalized communities a ready narratological structure to represent rebellion and collective transformation" (Mills 1997, 307). Similarly, for Robert Lang, "it is easy to see the attraction of gay filmmakers to the road movie genre, with all the possibilities it provides characters who choose to live and love outside the institution of the monogamous heterosexual partnership and the conventional nuclear family" (Lang 1997, 332). But are the spaces through which the protagonists of queer road movies pass the same as those traversed by the anti-heroes of *Easy Rider* (1969), *Two-Lane Blacktop* (1971), and *Vanishing Point* – and what is their interaction and association with that environment? Mills, in her analysis of *The Living End*, suggests that Jon and Luke "just don't have the relationship to the road, to the joy of mobility, or to the landscape which characterizes many road films." Although the couple ostensibly hit the road because Luke killed a cop, they are not pursued; as Mills suggests, their trip "becomes more like a vacation" than a rebellious rejection of conformity (Mills 1997, 311). It is unclear exactly what route Jon and Luke take during the film's narrative: aside from the brief sections of footage recorded in Texas by Richard Linklater, the film was shot in California, and when Jon and Luke end the film on a beach, it could be any of a number on the West Coast of the United States. (The scene was actually shot on Dockweiler State Beach, near LAX.) There is no footage of Nevada, Arizona, or New Mexico, which might have afforded the film more recognisable road movie landmarks. As Mills writes, "Their trip never takes them through the stock Western topography that symbolizes awesome eternity, like Monument Valley, but reveals only a postmodern wasteland of fast-food joints and ominous highway overpasses" (Mills 1997, 311).

The Living End has a fragile and partial relationship, then, to the generic form of the road movie, and this is evident in both narrative and aesthetic decisions. As David Laderman notes, as Jon and Luke's journey continues, "the film presents a series of night shots – unique for a road movie, which typically prefers glaring daylight on blacktop and desert surface" (Laderman 2002, 216). The boxy aspect ratio of the 16 mm frame stands in contrast to the widescreen aesthetics that are arguably more appropriate for the road film. Laderman also draws attention to *The Living End*'s "brazen use of tight close-ups": "More typically, the road movie uses extreme long shots to visually emphasize the characters passing through landscape." The "extra-tight framing," he argues, "conveys their claustrophobic enclosure in the car," but "also creates a space for their intimacy" (Laderman 2002, 216). And yet there are recognisable elements that clearly situate the film within the genre: bold skyscapes;

travelling shots recorded from a side window of the car; scenes in which Jon and Luke get to know each other, shot from the back seat, affording a view of the windscreen and the road along which they are driving.

Beyond the screwball comedy and the road movie, some commentators identify pornography as a key generic reference for *The Living End*. For Rich, Luke and Jon "could be characters out of a porn flick, the stud and the john, in a renegotiated terrain" (Rich 1992, 34). The actors who play the two lead roles were found through different means: Craig Gilmore (Jon) auditioned for the part, whereas Marcus Hu spotted Mike Dytri (Luke). Of the two, heterosexual Dytri had previous screen experience, having appeared in Forest Wise's film *Life Is Nice* (1991). Jon and Luke are presented as distinct physical types: the former, hirsute and thin, repeatedly plays with his floppy curtains of hair while covering his torso with oversized cardigans; the latter, chunky and often shirtless, is evidently comfortable in his unclothed frame. Dytri's body, shaped by years of training (he wrestled until college and spent many years competing in mixed martial arts), is aestheticized by Araki, in a manner that was inspired by Gus Van Sant: "*Mala Noche* [1986] is a film I saw before I wrote *The Living End* and the way Gus frames his male Adonises is very similar." The director also notes the influence of the late 1980s and early 1990s advertising aesthetic associated with photographers such as Herb Ritts and Bruce Weber: "That whole world of men being seen as sex objects and being lit and shot in a certain way was a huge influence on me" (Sproull 2022). In one shot of the sex scene between Luke and Ken, for instance, the camera looks up at Luke's face and pecs as he moves an unlit cigarette from his mouth to behind his ear. It then languorously moves down his body, the lighting emphasising a prominent vein in his bicep, eventually focusing on the white boxers he wears (figures 16–18). Luke pulls down his face-down partner's shorts and proceeds to spank him with a tennis racket: his is a phallic, active, and domineering masculinity.

Jon and Luke have a great deal of sex. More was scripted and shot, but ended up on the cutting-room floor, including an outdoors scene in which

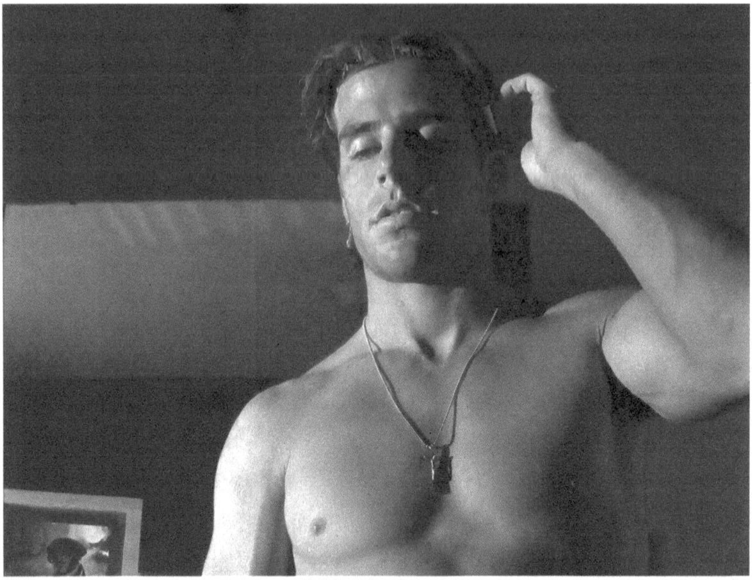

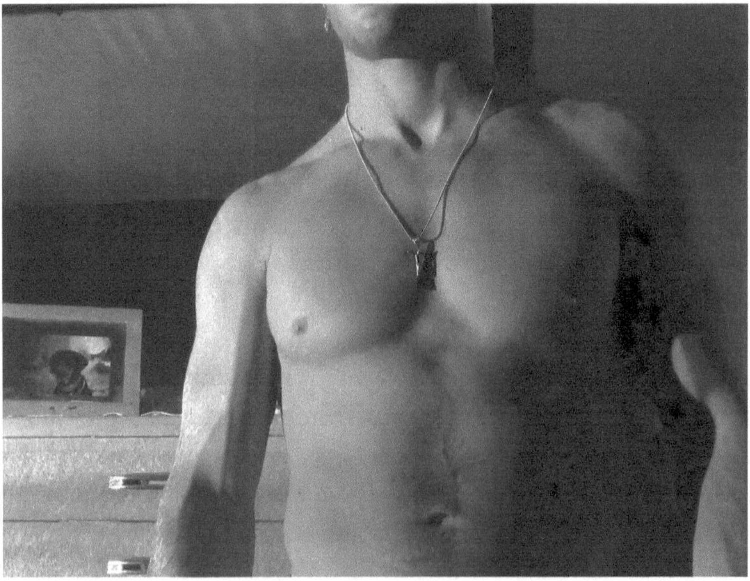

Figures 16, 17, and 18
Sexual spectacle: in one sex scene, the camera slowly drifts down Mike Dytri's body, lit to emphasize his musculature.

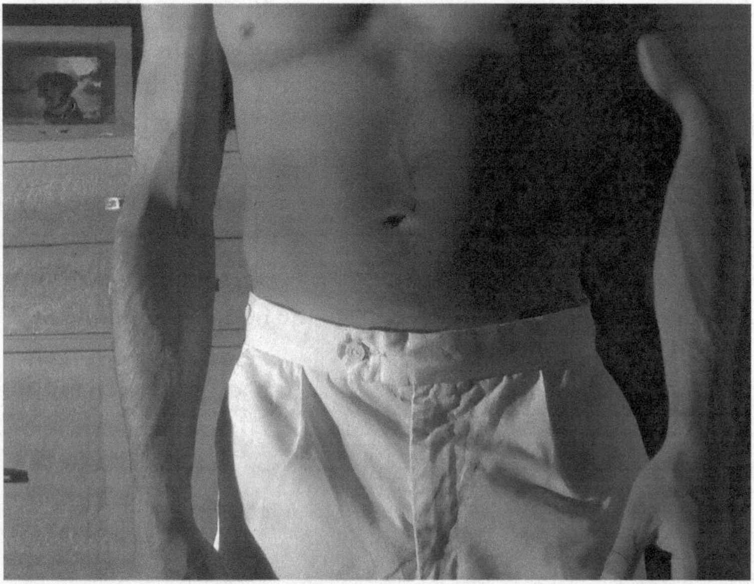

Luke squeezes chocolate syrup over Jon's naked torso and then licks it off him. "I'll never be able to eat a Hershey's Bar again without getting a hard-on," Jon says (Araki 1994, 65). Roy Grundmann describes the film as "largely a gay porn pastiche. Araki has studied his Halsted" (Grundmann 1993, 27). Fred Halsted's porn films – including *LA Plays Itself* (1972) and *Sextool* (1975) – depict explicit gay male sex, sometimes involving BDSM and (seemingly) non-consensual scenarios. Like *The Living End*, they imagine Los Angeles and its surrounding landscape as a playground for gay men to couple (and more) in. Unlike Halsted's films, however, the sex scenes in *The Living End* are discreetly shot and edited, the carnal action often out of frame or cut away from. When Luke seduces Jon, we do not witness the subsequent fuck. Later, as they grind together on a motel bed, their naked legs are relegated to the lower left corner of the frame, which instead draws attention to the room's chintzy curtains and the cartoon playing silently on a television (figure 19). Perhaps the most explicit (and "risky" or "irresponsible") scene involves the pair having sex in a shower. Jon fucks Luke without a condom, and during their coupling Luke asks Jon to choke him when he ejaculates. Despite the graphic talk and action, the camera, in medium close-up, stays above the waist (figure 20). Of course, it is worth recognising that, outside of actual porn, seeing two men have sex together on screen in 1992 was a rarity, especially at the height of the HIV epidemic. But Araki certainly had no intention of depicting explicit fucking: "I've never meant the nudity to be important to the film," he told Dale Reynolds.

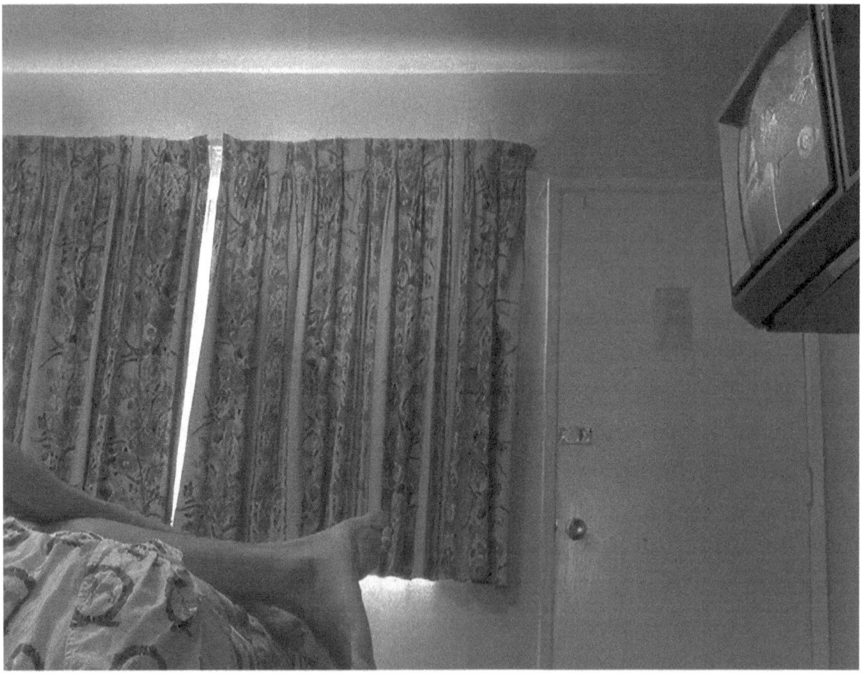

Figure 19
As Jon and Luke have sex in a motel, the framing relegates their fucking to the bottom left-hand corner of the frame.

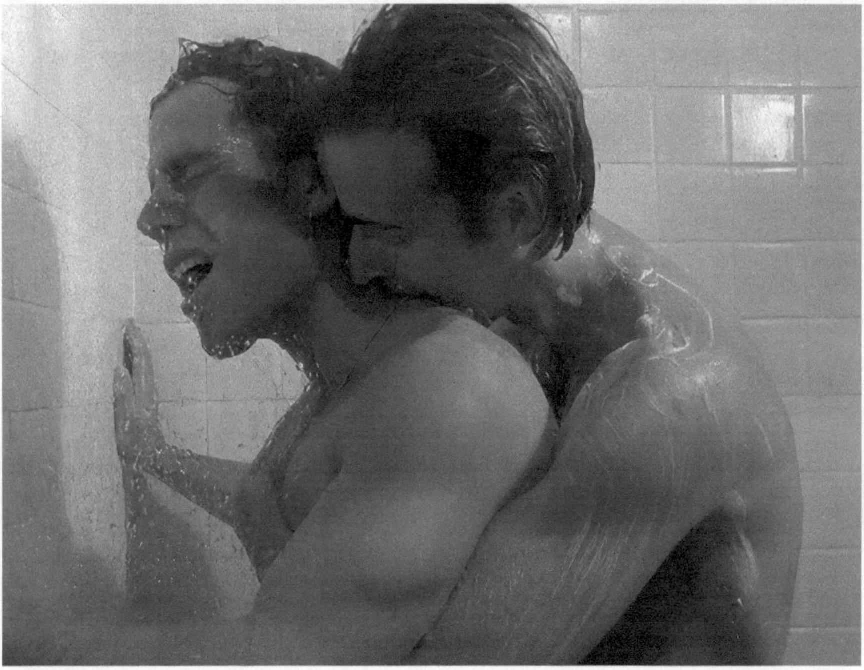

Figure 20
When Jon fucks Luke in the shower, the camera cuts off the action at waist height.

"Frankly, when sex is in the air, I'm much more interested in what's going on in the two men's heads than their dicks" (Reynolds 1993, 33). He expressed surprise that one criticism of the film was that "there should have been more flesh, that I should have shown Mike Dytri's cum shot" (Batrouney 1993, 67).

In the place of pornographic detail, what Araki does depict is an erotically charged physical intimacy. He repeatedly situates his camera close to Jon and Luke when they are teasing each other with foreplay, making out, or having sex, their faces filling the screen (figure 21). When Luke first seduces a shirtless Jon, he tells him that the thing he finds most attractive about men's bodies is

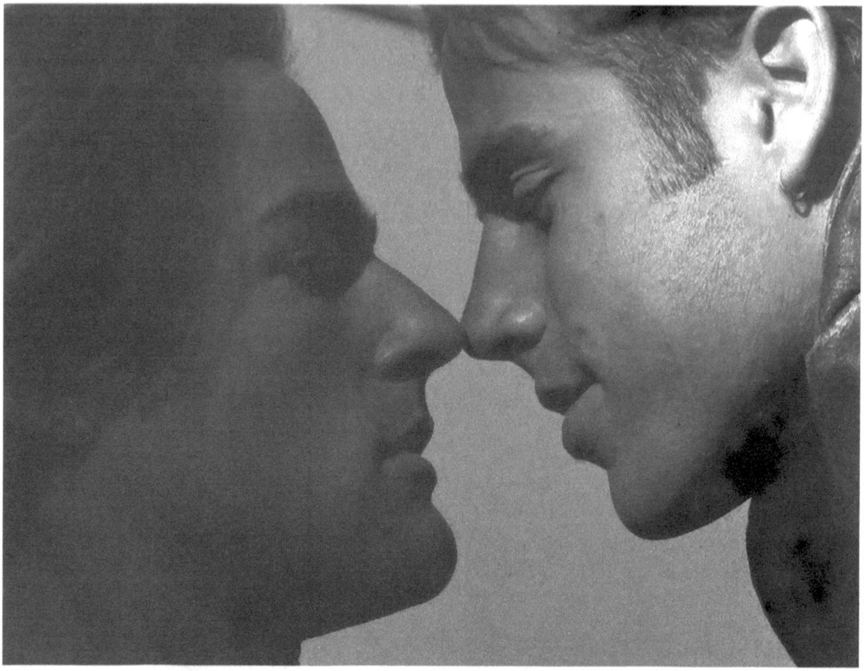

Figure 21
Araki's camera repeatedly establishes a physical intimacy with Jon and Luke.

the line that divides the torso from collarbone to belly. As Luke describes this physical feature, he traces his finger down Jon's chest, then softly kisses his stomach. Coming so soon after Jon's HIV diagnosis, this scene (like similar ones in *Buddies* and *Parting Glances*) asserts the power and necessity of sexual agency for HIV-positive men. As Luke Goodsell puts it, "The sex in *The Living End*, while explicit for the cinematic moment, is surprisingly tender, a respite from the horror of the world and a way for Jon and Luke to reclaim the chaos of their bodies" (Goodsell 2023). Even at the end of the film, following a sexual encounter in which Luke forces himself on Jon in public, the pair pull away from each other but quickly reunite, their physical closeness potentially forming a shield against their indeterminate future (figure 22).

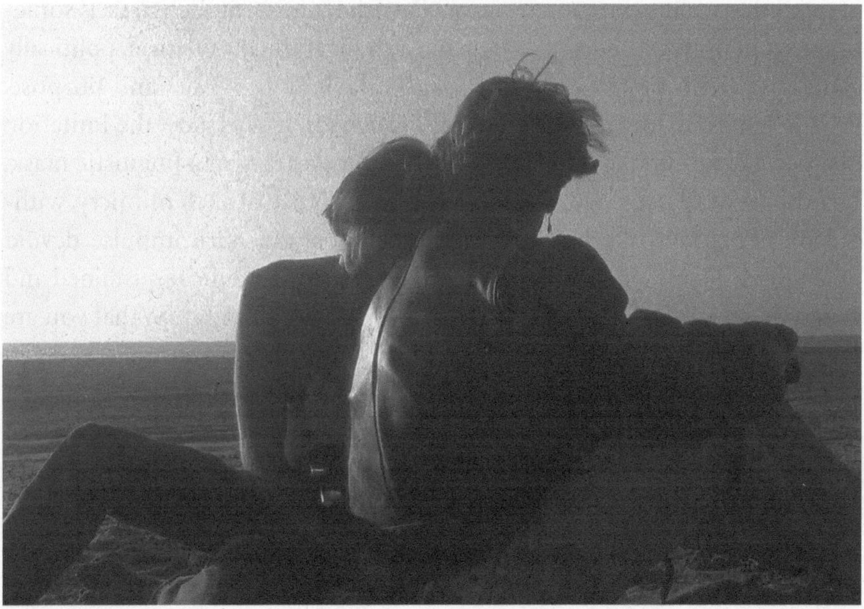

Figure 22
At the film's conclusion, the pair tenderly reunite as the sun sets over the ocean.

Appropriation, Pastiche, and Intertextuality

The Living End, then, borrows structural, narrative, and aesthetic elements from existing genres. This is part of what B. Ruby Rich means when she refers to New Queer Cinema films as defined by a "Homo Pomo" style, one marked by "traces of appropriation, pastiche, and irony." Araki's acts of appropriation are extensive: he repeatedly pilfers or references shots and scenes from other films. He also inserts explicit intertextual nods to an array of cultural texts through dialogue, props, and footage. What are we to make of this tapestry of quotations, allusions, borrowings? "Pastiche," the term Rich uses, is sometimes set in opposition to "parody"; the latter is framed as critical, politically generative, with pastiche its poor cousin, lacking in power and purpose. Fredric Jameson, for instance, writes: "Pastiche is, like parody, the imitation of a peculiar or unique, idiosyncratic style, the wearing of a linguistic mask, speech in a dead language. But it is a neutral practice of such mimicry, without any of parody's ulterior motives, amputated of the satiric impulse, devoid of laughter" (Jameson 1991, 32). Richard Dyer provides a more sustained and generous account of pastiche, defining it as "a kind of imitation that you are meant to know is an imitation" (Dyer 2007, 1). Pastiche involves a calculated artistic imitation of other art, often combining elements from various distinct sources. However, Dyer argues, it "is not something superficial, disconnected from the real and, especially, from feeling." Indeed, pastiche "always both holds us inexorably within cultural perception of the real and also, and thereby, enables us to make a sense of the real" (Dyer 2007, 2). Araki's acts of appropriation and intertextuality insert his films into a network of references: doffs of the cap to cherished antecedents and peers, and sassy (and sometimes unexpected) citations. They invite the viewer to take pleasure in recognised nods, and to undertake subsequent detective work into missed or unknown allusions. But they also gesture to an artistic goal shared by Araki and the creators of many of his pastiched referents: an attempt to make sense of the world, to capture and dissect the mood of a moment, to envision moral and political alternatives to the status quo. There is not room here to unpack all of the allusions in *The Living End*, but a sample can provide useful insights into Araki's methods and results.

Araki's love of Jean-Luc Godard has already been mentioned in the introduction to this book. Jon and Luke, the protagonists of *The Living End*, are so named in honour of the French director. Jon's apartment has a number of film posters (that we see), one of which is for Godard's *Made in USA* (1966). Besides a screening at the 1967 New York Film Festival, this movie was not officially released in the United States for over four decades due to legal action.

Jon's poster thus depicts a lost object, a sought-after but elusive work that only circulated somewhat illicitly and thus developed a particular subterranean cachet. In Jon's apartment, Luke picks up some magazine pages and papers that Jon is using to write an essay on "The Death of Cinema." Among them are a portrait of Godard and a flyer featuring Derek Jarman's name. Godard repeatedly made pronouncements on the death of cinema, which he envisaged as due to: a slump or suppression of the medium after the innovations of the silent era; its inability to confront the horrors of the Holocaust; its calcification (post-May 1968) as a reactionary cultural form; and so on (see Witt 1999). Jon's reference to the "death of cinema" is another in *The Living End*'s litany of references to death (discussed in the previous chapter). It may also suggest, following one of Godard's arguments, that cinema is not an adequate medium for dealing with the horrors of the widespread and incomprehensible loss caused by HIV/AIDS.

As I noted above, though not mentioned in *The Living End*, Araki references Godard's film *Pierrot le Fou* (1965) in publicity materials and interviews as an influence.[2] The main connection between the two films is generic: like *The Living End*, *Pierrot le Fou* riffs on the "lovers on the run" movie. In Godard's film, Ferdinand (Jean-Paul Belmondo) flees from his wife, kids, and middle-class life with his ex-girlfriend Marianne (Anna Karina), and the two go on a crime spree that takes them from the metropolis to the Mediterranean. The ending of Godard's film differs from Araki's: Marianne betrays Ferdinand, and he kills her and then blows himself up. Beyond the generic link, there are also aesthetic connections: *Pierrot le Fou* uses bold swathes of colour, of carefully crafted minimal set design, of advertising signs and posters. Further, Godard was quoted as saying that "all you need to make a movie is a girl and a gun," though he himself attributed the line to D.W. Griffith; the dangerous, irresponsible girl with a gun in *Pierrot le Fou* is a boy in Araki's film, though he causes similar levels of havoc.

A second poster in Jon's apartment is for a season of Andy Warhol films – possibly a West Coast iteration of the 1988 programme coordinated by the

Whitney Museum in New York. The poster features several frames from *Blow Job* (1964), Warhol's structuralist silent black-and-white work that runs for just over thirty minutes. *Blow Job* depicts DeVeren Bookwalter's starkly lit head and neck as, out of frame, he possibly receives the titular pleasure.[3] Or is he acting? As with Warhol's other cinematic experiments with slowness, stillness, and duration from around this time (such as *Eat*, *Empire*, and *Henry Geldzahler*, all 1964), *Blow Job* was filmed at 24 frames per second (fps) but projected at 16 fps, giving it an oneiric, spacey quality. The title of Warhol's film advertises it as potentially pornographic, but *Blow Job* fails to deliver any explicit content; similarly, as previously noted, *The Living End*'s sex scenes are all delicately framed and edited. As Jon enters his apartment early on in the film, he cranes his head backwards, stretching out the day's stresses, and his posture recalls Bookwalter's (figure 23). Expunged from its narrative surroundings, this single shot could seem to imply he was being fellated. Araki's debt to Warhol surfaces elsewhere in *The Living End*, in his casting of Factory regular Mary Woronov as one of the lesbian murderers. Woronov, who appears in a number of Warhol's films including *Chelsea Girls* and *Since* (both 1966), brings to Araki's film a performance style associated with underground and avant-garde cinema. I will return to this acting mode shortly.[4]

A third poster, relatively small, is for Jon Moritsugu's first feature film *My Degeneration* (1989). Made for $5,000 and only an hour in length, the lo-fi film charts the rise and fall of an all-girl rock band that becomes a pawn of the beef industry. David Fear, writing in *Rolling Stone*, describes *My Degeneration* as "a scuzzy, 16mm skullfuck opus," one that "*feels* like punk rock: dirty, angry, righteous, handmade, exhilarating" (Grierson et al. 2021). As Jun Okada notes, all of Moritsugu's films "riff on variations of the mod teen film genre." They are "full of disaffected youth, lengthy punk rock music performances, luridly meandering exploitation plots and subplots, and special effects more reminiscent of Russ Meyer than Wayne Wang" (Okada 2015, 71–2). As I identified in chapter 1, Araki's films have sometimes been linked to Moritsugu's, in that both are Asian American filmmakers who work outside of the norms

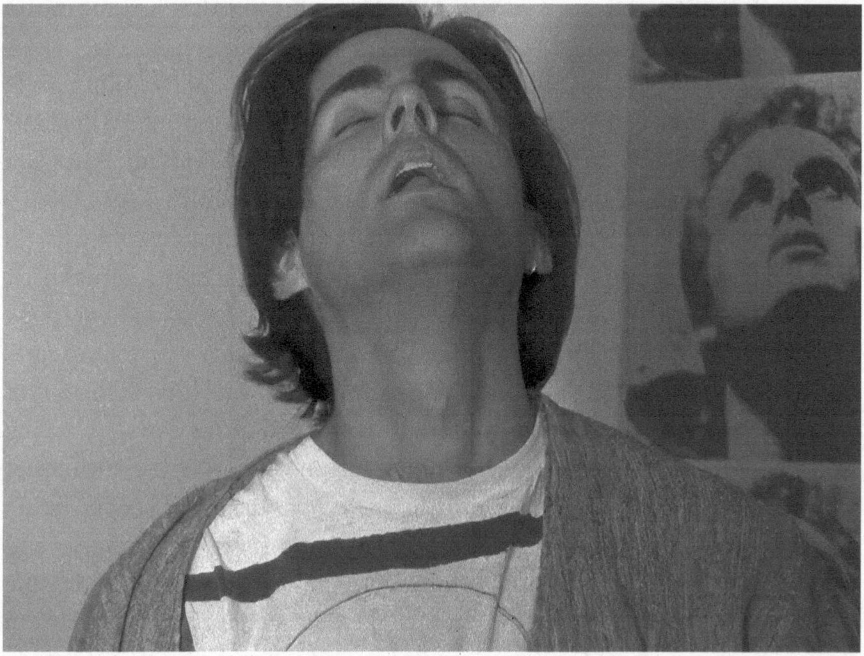

Figure 23
Jon's posture mimics that of DeVeren Bookwalter in Andy Warhol's film *Blow Job* (1964).

and expectations of independent Asian American cinema, and who are invested in underground musical and sexual subcultures. As Moritsugu puts it, "Within the [Asian American] community itself, both my films, Gregg [Araki]'s films, and the [films of] a few other filmmakers such as Roddy Bogawa, are seen as rebellious youthful punk-rock products … We're looked upon in a hostile way by a lot of people in the Asian American community because they feel we've forsaken our heritage, our roots" (Okada 2015, 71). Not only does Araki nod to Moritsugu through the poster in *The Living End*, but he features an extract from Moritsugu's film *Hippy Porn* (1991) in *Totally F***ed Up*: Steven (Gilbert Luna) and Deric (Lance May) watch the film while

Tommy (Roko Belic) dozes next to them. "This is the weirdest fucking movie I've ever seen," says Steven.[5]

Beyond the social and cultural connections between the two filmmakers that the inclusion of this poster represents, what does it contribute to the film? For Jon, it represents an aesthetic distinct from that of Godard (European "new wave" arthouse) and Warhol (American structuralist experiment): Moritsugu's films are noisy, abrasive, vulgar, unhinged. Jon's cinephilic tastes are flagged as diverse, manifold. But there are additional semiotic resonances. The title of Moritsugu's film obviously riffs on the name of the 1965 song "My Generation" by the Who, the rebellious lyrics of which welcome an early demise before predicted decrepitude or fading in old age. Jon is scornful of such immature celebrations of youthful death and annihilation. Driving around Los Angeles soon after receiving the results of his HIV test, he intones into his Dictaphone: "'Live fast, die young, leave a beautiful corpse.' Yeah, right." For Jon's generation of young gay men, youthful death from HIV and AIDS is a very real and unwelcome prospect. The "degeneration" in the title of Moritsugu's film becomes, in *The Living End*, a suggestion or intimation of bodily deterioration: for HIV-positive Jon and Luke, the future is likely to be one of inevitable painful physical decline.

These Godard, Warhol, and Moritsugu posters, all in close proximity to one another, are joined by a fourth filmic reference point: a human-height inflatable model of Godzilla. Though this could initially seem like a disposable trinket, merely an amusing object with which to decorate a space, it serves as a further intertextual nod. Again, it suggests the breadth of Jon's cinematic tastes (as global and not limited to instances of films with elitist or subcultural cachet). It serves as yet another signifier in *The Living End* of death and destruction: across the many films in which the character has appeared, Godzilla often wantonly razes cities, putting the lives of their inhabitants in peril. Ishiro Honda's original 1954 film can be seen as an allegory of the atomic bomb strikes suffered by Hiroshima and Nagasaki in August 1945, with the devastation caused by the reptilian creature serving as an echo of the impact caused by the bombings. *Godzilla*'s vision of furious, out-of-control nature randomly wreaking revenge on human populations could find a parallel in common narratives of HIV: cause debated and indistinct; resistant to standard methods of scientific attack; localised impact, but with the threat of further spread; significant and ruthless slaughter caused; potentially unstoppable. Luke may playfully punch Godzilla in the head, but the beast bounces back.

Araki's borrowings and references certainly index his catholic tastes. In a 2022 interview, he revealed that the final scene of *The Living End* was influenced by the conclusion of *The Graduate* (1967). He tried to capture "that *Graduate* moment of just total uncertainty – like, what's going to happen now?" ("Pioneers" 2022). At the end of the Mike Nichols film, Benjamin (Dustin Hoffman) interrupts Elaine's (Katharine Ross) marriage to Carl (Brian Avery), and the two abscond together. Sitting at the back of a bus, Elaine still in her bridal gown, their gleeful expressions fall as they realise the gravity of what they have done. As I identified in the previous chapter, the conclusion of *The Living End* refuses the standard narrative AIDS death for Jon and Luke: they have to face their unclear future together as HIV-positive men. Some of Araki's borrowings in *The Living End* are from queer forebears, paying homage to key figures such as Warhol. Others are from peers, such as Moritsugu. Yet others are from surprisingly canonical heterosexual cinephilic sources: Nichols, Godard, Hawks. These last sources are not necessarily being "queered," though their use certainly reveals how the elements plundered from them can find a home in an overtly queer text. Rather, it perhaps makes more sense, as Eve Oishi argues, to see Araki's magpie method as one that is in itself "irresponsible," involving "a deliberate identification with avant-garde practices and sensibilities, which are understood as and through a frustration of mainstream aesthetic and generic conventions as well as a frustration of ideological readings that assume a link between artistic expression and personal identity or politics" (Oishi 2017, 112). As I noted in chapter 1, Araki is a "nerdy" film buff who has often rebuffed community allegiances (indeed, Rich calls him "the bad boy of New Queer Cinema" [Rich 2013, 92]). He mixes and matches his stolen materials – classical mainstream with no-budget scuzz, heterosexual romcom with smutty queer underground experiment – into a tapestry pastiche in the service of advancing his tales and perspective. The motley array of his referenced sources reveals not only the complex operations of his often-surprising tastes, but the configuration of a highly specific metaphysics, a dissident cosmology.

Mise-en-Scène

Writing about Araki's first two films, *Three Bewildered People in the Night* and *The Long Weekend (O' Despair)*, Daryl Chin praises their "compositional boldness" and draws attention to the director's attraction "to the quality of light within the artificially lit urban landscape" (Chin 1993, 106). With the move to colour that occurred with *The Living End*, Araki's frame arrangements and sensitivity to the drama of effective lighting (both nocturnal and diurnal) became enriched with a dynamic pop palette. The first thirty seconds of the film evidence these new brash colour choices: the title appears, static, against a blood red background; this red is echoed in the spray paint Luke is using to graffiti the words "fuck the world"; and then our first sight of Luke positions him against a pure Californian sky. Strong reds and blues recur across the film: Luke's encounter with the psychotic lesbians pits their red car against the blue sky; Luke scrawls "I Blame Society" in a car park lit in a rich blue hue; Ken and Barbie's bedroom is a claret red, which Barbie's red dress and elbow-length gloves echo – as does Ken's spilled blood after Barbie stabs him. Beyond these colours, the palette is rich and varied, as Araki demonstrates a pop and Godardian understanding of dynamic and memorable image composition.

One of the most distinctive aspects of Araki's cinema is his choice of locations, both exterior and interior. As Chris Chang writes, "There is something quintessentially LA about an Araki film, but there are no recognizable landmarks" (Chang 1994, 50). The director's selection of exteriors is dominated by storefronts, petrol stations, advertising hoardings, and parking garages, with particular locations chosen for the dramatic framing or valuable commentary they afford. (There is possibly a connection to be made between Ed Ruscha's fascination with gasoline stations and Araki's depictions of similar locations.) Jon and Luke's encounter with the neo-Nazi when they are shopping takes place outside Soap Plant, the store's corner pillar painted with flames which accentuate the scene's heated exchange (figure 24). Later, the pair stock up on supplies at an ampm mini market, and Luke ignores a "Don't Drink and Drive" sign and tips a bottle of Jack Daniel's into a green plastic container with a straw (figure 25). A couple of kooks declaim an extract from a legislative document outside a 7-Eleven. They are squashed into the bottom left corner of the shot, while the top of the frame is dominated by a billboard for a Western wear chain with the slogan, "Think of them as hush puppies in heat," words which seem to comment on both the cowboy boots depicted and the pair's eccentric behaviour (figure 26). On the road, Jon and Luke are framed near or against a series of striking retro signs: Mike's (figure 27); a drive-in liquor and cheque-cashing store (figure 28); Circus Liquor (figure 29). These signs are evidence of the gaudy industrial anachronistic detritus that litters the Californian landscape.

Araki combines these exteriors with carefully choreographed interior sets. Take, for instance, Jon's trip to the doctor for the result of his HIV test. Jon, wearing a grey cardigan over a T-shirt depicting Jesus, sits below a poster of the female reproductive system. The doctor dismissively delivers the results ("positive; sorry") as he grinds out a cigarette in an ashtray. The doctor is played by Mark Finch, a vital figure in the history of queer cinema in the UK and the US. He was a driving force behind the founding of the London Lesbian and Gay Film Festival, wrote several groundbreaking scholarly essays on queer film and television, and, having moved from London to San Francisco, was hired as the exhibitions and festival director for Frameline, helping to run the city's International Lesbian and Gay Film Festival in the early 1990s. Asked by *Capital Gay* newspaper about the cameo role, Araki refers to Finch as an

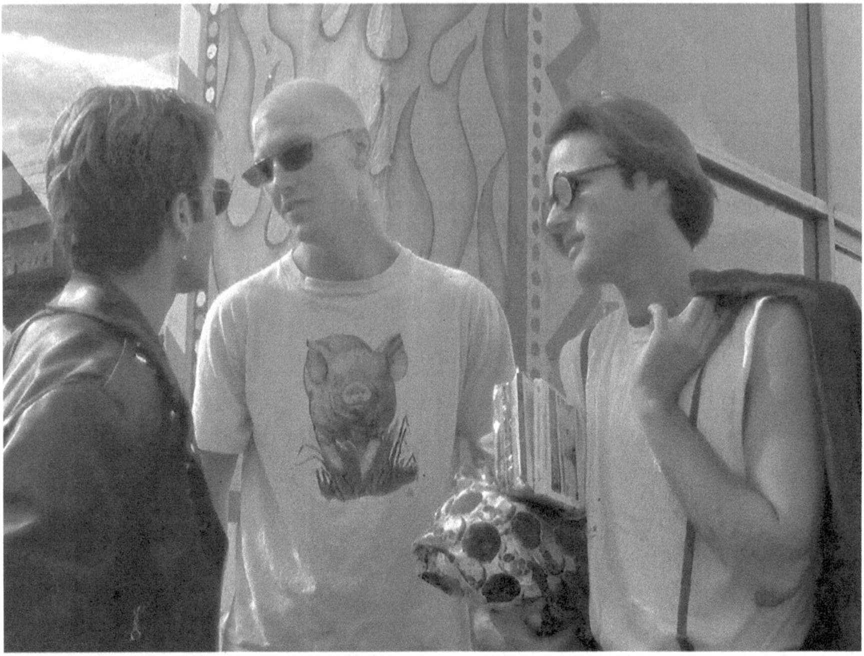

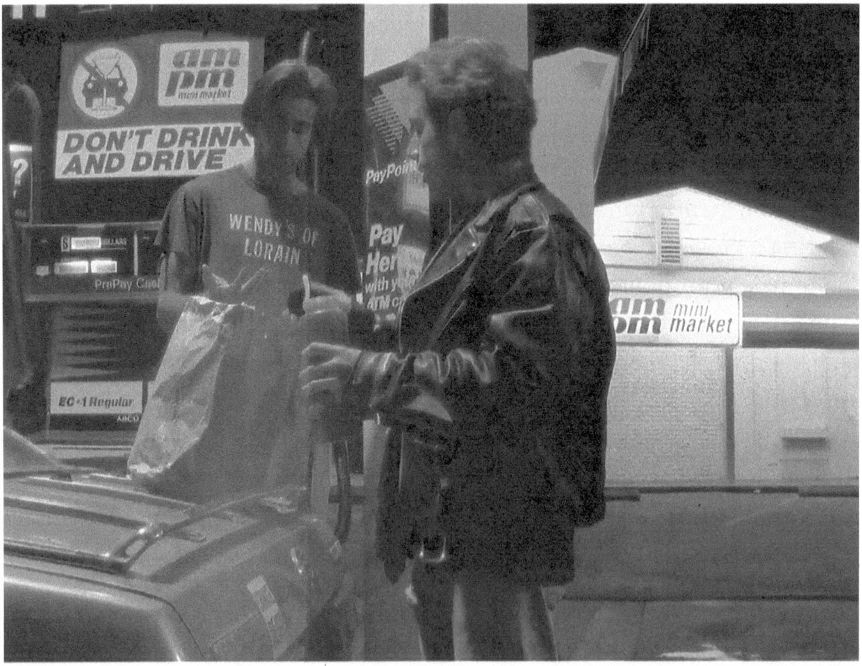
am pm mini market
DON'T DRINK AND DRIVE
WENDY'S OF LORAIN
EC-1 Regular
am pm mini market

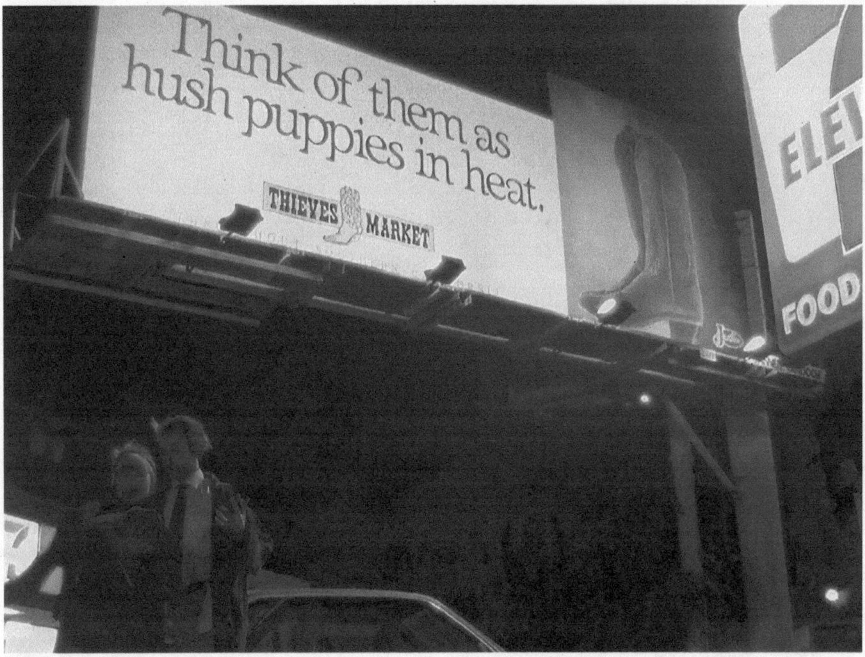

Figures 24, 25, and 26
Araki's exterior locations sometimes emphasize, pass ironic commentary on, or suggest interpretation of the film's narrative.

"underground superstar" (Stimpson 1993, 9). The gravity of this scene – which sets the narrative of the film rolling – is undermined somewhat by the set design decisions. Finch wears an inappropriately jazzy marine-blue-and-white patterned shirt underneath his white coat; a Herb Ritts beefcake poster hangs on the wall, next to further anatomical posters relating to fertility and pregnancy; chunky pieces of technology, including a computer, are generously embellished with sticky notes; sitting on the desk are a hip flask, the ashtray, an issue of *LA Style*, and a skull with rickety lower teeth (figure 30). If this is a doctor's office, it is an unconventional one, cluttered with bric-a-brac and

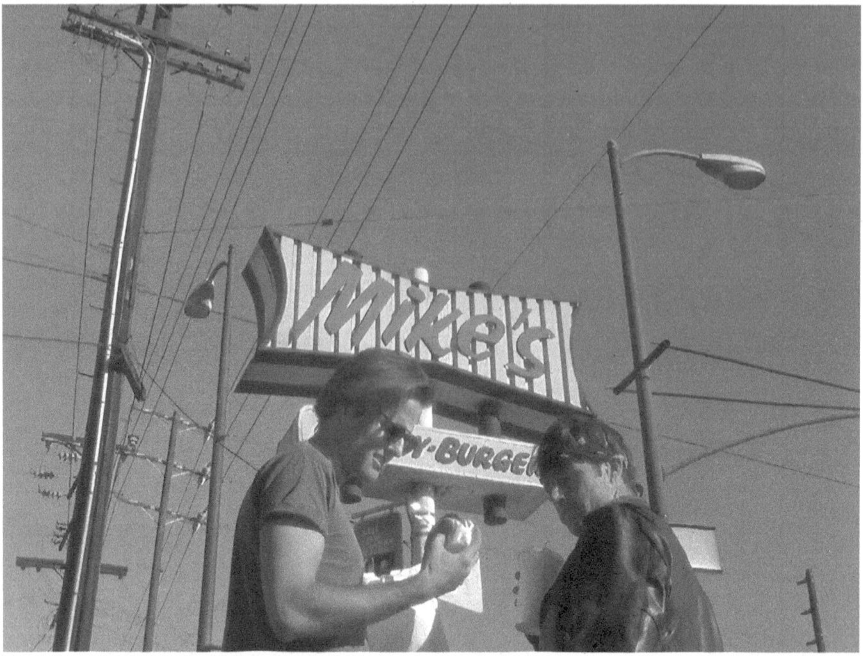
Mike's

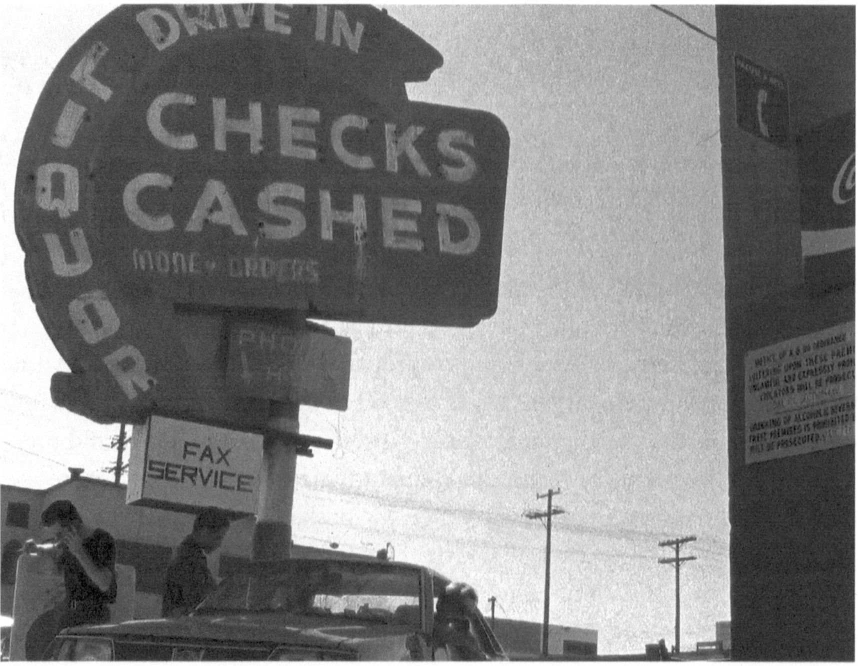
DRIVE IN
LIQUOR
CHECKS
CASHED
FAX
SERVICE

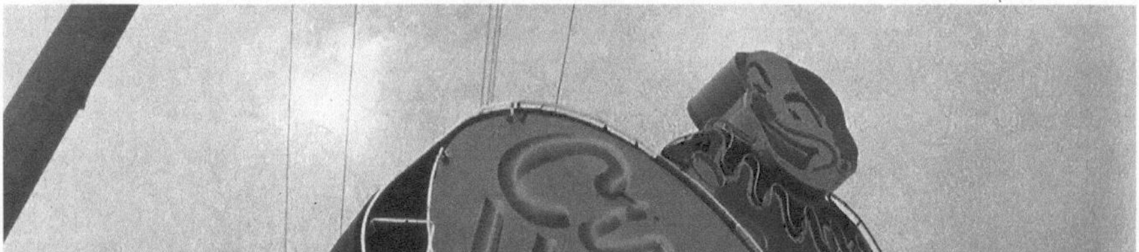

Figures 27, 28, and 29
At other times, Araki selects exterior locations for their aesthetic impact: *The Living End* features an array of retro signs.

indicators of poor health practices. Homoerotic art jars against markers of healthy childbearing.

Many of the interior locations and props deployed in *The Living End* were simply sourced from the cast and crew: Jon's Subaru and many of the band T-shirts belonged to Araki; Darcy and Jon's apartments were those of Marcus Hu and Andrea Sperling. The three homophobes shot by Luke wear T-shirts emblazoned with the words "Drugstore Cowboy," "sex, lies, and videotape," and "Avenue Pictures," which (as noted in chapter 1) were provided by Sperling, who had been an intern at Avenue. However, Araki's broader prop use reveals a camp appreciation for disposable pop culture ephemera. Twice in

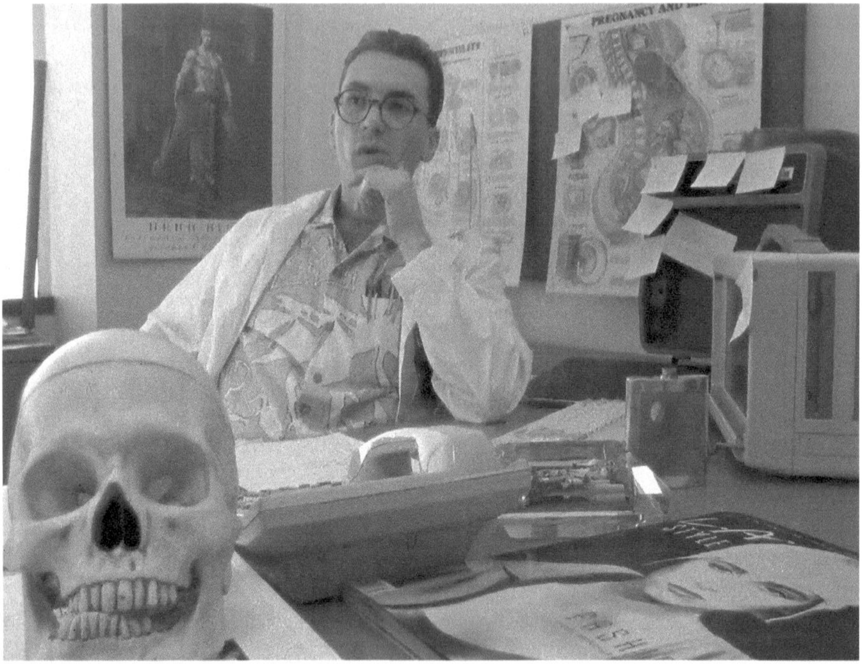

Figure 30
The doctor's office, cluttered with bric-a-brac, highlights Araki's magpie mise-en-scène choices.

his apartment, Jon stands on a squeaky toy shaped like a butt. Darcy occasionally passes the time clapping her hands to stir a response from a sound-activated mechanical rubber fish. Next to his answerphone, Jon has a retro robot toy and an unusable comedy mug with a sharp metal rod sticking up out of its base that reads, "Ask me about my lobotomy" (figure 31). Both Darcy and Jon have mannequins or mannequin parts in their homes, Darcy's painted in a mottled black-and-white pattern (figure 32). These accumulated knick-knacks provide additional colour to the film's aesthetic, but also suggest that the film's characters take a gleeful pop pleasure in trashy objects.

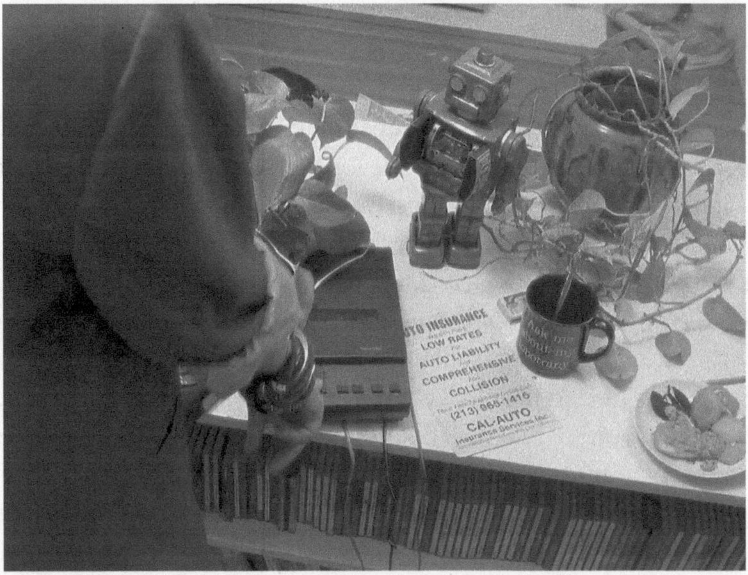

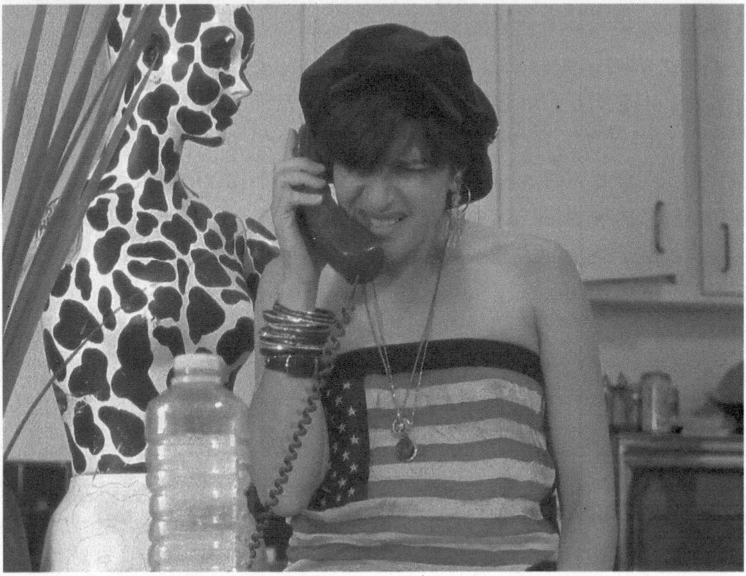

Figures 31 and 32
Araki and his characters take delight in pop culture ephemera, from retro robots to clothing mannequins.

At heightened physical and emotional moments in the narrative, stylistic excesses are sometimes stripped back. As Jon's doctor provides standard advice about safer sex for "high risk" groups, we see (but do not hear) Jon vomiting in a plain institutional toilet cubicle. After fleeing from Ken's home, Luke pauses in a parking lot under a buzzing light. A close-up captures him, unlit cigarette between his lips, as he catches his breath and recovers. Jon and Luke's shower fuck takes place against plain white tiling, accentuating the coupling of their naked bodies. At the film's conclusion, when Luke fucks Jon, the beach is deserted, the location reduced to sand, sea, and sky. After the encounter, as the pair face their future together, the sun begins to set and the sky turns an orange-pink hue, Jon and Luke demoted to tiny figures within the frame. Araki's mise-en-scène choices in *The Living End*, then, evidence what Rich refers to as New Queer Cinema's "alternately minimalist and excessive" style: he makes space for both clutter and its absence.

Rich's "minimalist and excessive" designation could also be applied to the performance styles in *The Living End*. Araki draws a distinction between the film's four main characters – Jon and Luke, Darcy and her boyfriend Peter – and all of the others. As I noted in this book's introduction, Araki told Mansel Stimpson that "all of the supporting characters regardless of gender or sexual orientation are presented in a garish, almost cartoonish, satirical way" (Stimpson 1993, 9). In conversation with Dale Reynolds, Araki elaborates on this point: Jon and Luke, he states, inhabit a "surreal" and "over the top" environment peopled with "bizarre figures who threaten the characters": "the film is populated with a world of weirdos ... Jon, Luke, Darcy, Peter, those characters are real" (Reynolds 1993, 34). Certainly, the register of the performances of Johanna Went and Mary Woronov (Daisy and Fern), of Nicole Dillenberg (Barbie) and Christopher Mabli (the neo-Nazi), is distinct from those of the two main couples. With these smaller roles, the acting is more theatrical, campy, crude, performative. As previously highlighted, this performance style is redolent of many of Andy Warhol's semi-scripted films, John Waters's films of the 1960s and 1970s, George Kuchar's parodies of Hollywood melodrama, and many other films associated with the queer and punk undergrounds. The impact of these bit parts is to reveal the artifice of the fiction we are watching, to draw attention to its constructed and scripted form – and thus to flag up that the "realistic" characters are also performers occupying roles. Indeed, perhaps Araki's distinction between the two central character pairs and the supporting cast is not so clear-cut. Amanda Howell comments that the conversation between Jon and Luke over breakfast is "less a naturalistic exchange of ideas between two psychologized characters than a series of slogans, suitable for T-shirts or bumper stickers"; in this, it is "like much of the film's dialogue" (Howell 2015, 133). Certainly, the speech of most of the characters in *The Living End* tends towards aphorisms and non-sequiturs, but this does not mean that Jon and Luke, Jon and Darcy, and Darcy and Peter do not have some genuine, quiet moments of intimacy, of shared companionship, of sparring banter. For all of the artifice on display, the film's romanticism is necessarily lodged in its depictions of gentle and affectionate kinship.

Music and Soundtrack

In an "Industry Talk" interview with Araki at Sundance London in 2023, the director was asked whether a particular director or film had been a pivotal influence on his career. He replied: "There's a lot of filmmakers that have influenced me and been inspirations for me, but never one that I feel changed my life. And what actually changed my life, the biggest factor for me, was … music – and particularly British music … The Cure, the Smiths, Siouxsie and the Banshees, Gang of Four, all of it – all of that music really shaped my sensibility, it shaped my view" ("Gregg Araki Industry Talk" 2023). The influence was not just the music made by the bands but their philosophical approach: many were not concerned with mainstream appeal, invested rather in following their own creative impulses. Araki's taste in music saturates his films, providing them with a particular register and patina. His signature sound is a combination of industrial music (bands such as KMFDM, Coil, Babyland, and 16Volt) and shoegaze (Cocteau Twins, Slowdive, Curve, Ride, Pale Saints), with some sonic space afforded to other mainstream and indie pop. As his budgets increased from *The Doom Generation* (1995) onwards, he has been increasingly able to license music by bands he was previously unable to afford. Across his career, Araki has been known to provide his actors with compilation tapes and lyric sheets in order to help them better locate and understand their characters. Araki's love of music has manifested through other channels: in the late 1980s, he was a reviewer for *LA Weekly*. As he tells Madeline Frino, "Every day was like Christmas, because you'd get all these new records in the mail … I think I made like 25 cents a word, but it was a really cool experience to be a part of the music press for a bit. I interviewed The Jesus and Mary Chain, who were at the peak of Jesus and Mary Chain-ness" (Frino 2024).

The title of *The Living End* is actually taken from a song by the Jesus and Mary Chain.[6] Although "The Living End" does not appear in the film, the band provides a point of connection between Luke and Jon: Luke wears a Jesus and Mary Chain T-shirt in the film's opening scene, and there are two posters for the band's debut album *Psychocandy* (1985) in Jon's apartment (one on the wall, the other in the closet; the latter is blink-and-you'll-miss-it). The songs on *Psychocandy* married classic Phil Spector–style pop structures and melodies with abrasive guitar noise and piercing feedback. "The Living End," its second track, is about a narcissistic biker taking pleasure in his own appearance and driving at speed at night; at the conclusion he meets a bloody end by crashing into a tree. The song seems to provide a voice to the idolised figure at the centre of the 1964 single "Leader of the Pack" by the Shangri-Las. Both songs romanticise and eulogise the rebel biker – an archetype incarnated on screen, in particular, by Marlon Brando in *The Wild One* (1953). There is a self-obsessed, dark erotic tinge to "The Living End": the biker figure at the heart of the song could have stepped out of Kenneth Anger's film *Scorpio Rising* (1963). In Araki's film, "lonesome cowboy" Luke, adrift across America, lacks a motorcycle but does own a leather jacket and shades. Like Johnny, Brando's character in *The Wild One*, he ends his narrative alive but facing an uncertain future.

In addition to "The Living End," which Araki envisioned opening his film, the director had a clear idea of the music that he wanted to feature. The published screenplay names specific artists and songs to be used with particular scenes: "There Is a Light that Never Goes Out" by the Smiths, "Coast to Coast" by the Jesus and Mary Chain, "Flashback" and "Burning Inside" by Ministry, "Faith and Healing" by Ian McCulloch, "Thieves Like Us" by New Order. None of these appear in the completed film, but were evidently inspirations and aspirations. Indeed, bands that Araki reveres feature in a number of places in *The Living End* as allusions, but not as audio. Early in the film, Jon narrates into his Dictaphone: "Stopped off at Aron's and bought the new Dead Can Dance CD. Got the results of my first AIDS test." (Aron's Records was an independent store in Los Angeles that opened in 1965 and closed in 2006.) In Jon's apartment, a large tour poster for the Smiths hangs over the kitchen table (figure 33); Luke, at one point when he and Jon are on the road, uses the line, "What difference does it make?," possibly a reference to the Smiths song of the same title. (In *Totally F***ed Up*, one character delivers the line "shyness is nice," a quotation from "Ask" by the Smiths.) Luke wears an array of band T-shirts throughout the film, including Ministry and Misfits. Peter comments to Darcy that Jon "went into severe depression for two weeks when Echo and the Bunnymen broke up." When Darcy listens to Jon's answerphone messages, he has missed calls about Revolting Cocks tickets and an errant Nitzer Ebb CD. Howell suggests that the most significant of the musical references in *The Living End* is to Joy Division. After telling Darcy about his test results, Jon says, "I need to lay off those Joy Division records for a while." The Psychic TV song "I.C. Water," a tribute to Joy Division vocalist Ian Curtis, features on the soundtrack. Whilst on the road, Jon and Luke discuss Curtis's suicide; this is accompanied, as Howell notes, by "roadside images of

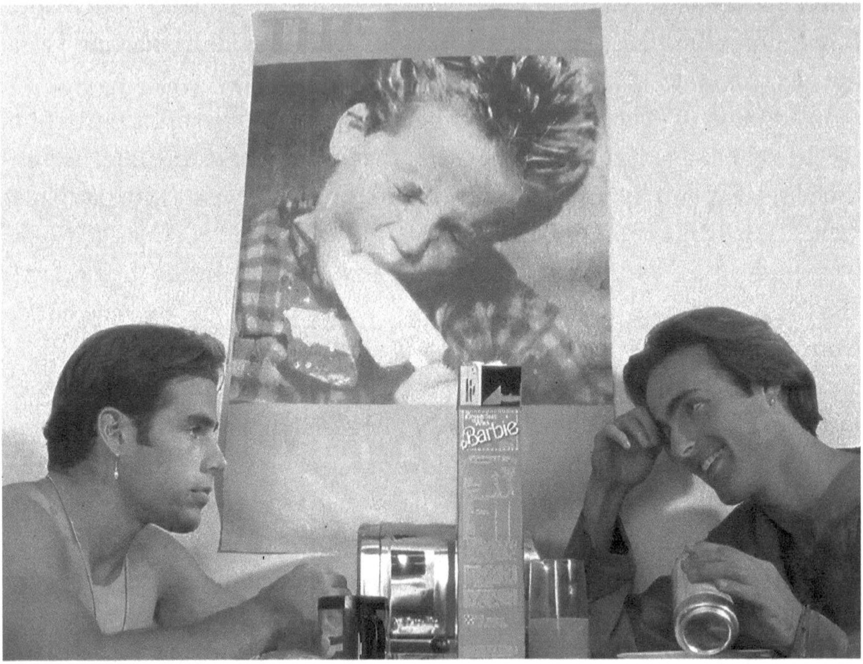

Figure 33
References to post-punk and indie music proliferate across *The Living End*, as with a poster for the Smiths above Jon's kitchen table.

a seemingly alien landscape" which "offer the visual correlative of the 'bleak soundscapes' of Joy Division's music" (Howell 2015, 133). All of these references to particular bands, peppered across the film, construct a shared world of indie/post-punk/goth/industrial music that connects the characters and (arguably) the film's audience.

Perhaps one of the most surprising references in the film appears as a subtle detail. On the windowsill in Jon's apartment is a seven-inch record of the Roberta Flack song "Making Love" (1982) (figure 34). This gooey ballad –

written by Burt Bacharach, Bruce Roberts, and Carole Bayer Sager – was the theme song for the film of the same name and reached number thirteen in the US Billboard Hot 100. *Making Love* was a mainstream Hollywood attempt to tackle the topic of homosexuality: the 20th Century Fox film starred Michael Ontkean as Zack, an oncologist who leaves his wife Claire (Kate Jackson) when a series of encounters with Bart (Harry Hamlin) forces him to confront and act on his desires for other men. The film's trailer warned audiences about its content: "*Making Love* deals openly and candidly with a delicate issue. It is not sexually explicit. But it may be too strong for some people." The film might now seem tame and somewhat soapy, but it was a landmark instance of mainstream "positive imagery." Significantly, it also appeared in cinemas the year after HIV began to hit gay communities in North America. New Queer Cinema, of course, rebelled against films such as *Making Love*, with their anodyne depictions of lesbian and gay characters. The film would certainly not appeal to Jon, fan of Godard, Moritsugu, and Warhol. Further, the musical style of Flack's "Making Love" is at a significant remove from all of the other music that *The Living End* alludes to or features. Perhaps, for those who notice it, we are supposed to see the single as a goofy or ironic choice, akin to the lobotomy mug or the skeleton in the closet; or possibly it represents a guilty pleasure.

The genre that actually dominates the soundtrack of *The Living End* is industrial. Several of the bands that feature on it – Psychic TV, Fred, Coil, Chris & Cosey – had connections to the experimental industrial group Throbbing Gristle, which was known for its challenging and confrontational records and performances. These four bands were all on Wax Trax! Records, one of the main industrial labels – as were Braindead Sound Machine, Cambodia, and KMFDM, whose music also appears in Araki's film. Industrial music, as Howell notes, "emphasized noise experiments (tape loops, sampling, white noise, spoken word performance) calculated to resist commercial co-optation … while communicating a critical view of the world that industrialization

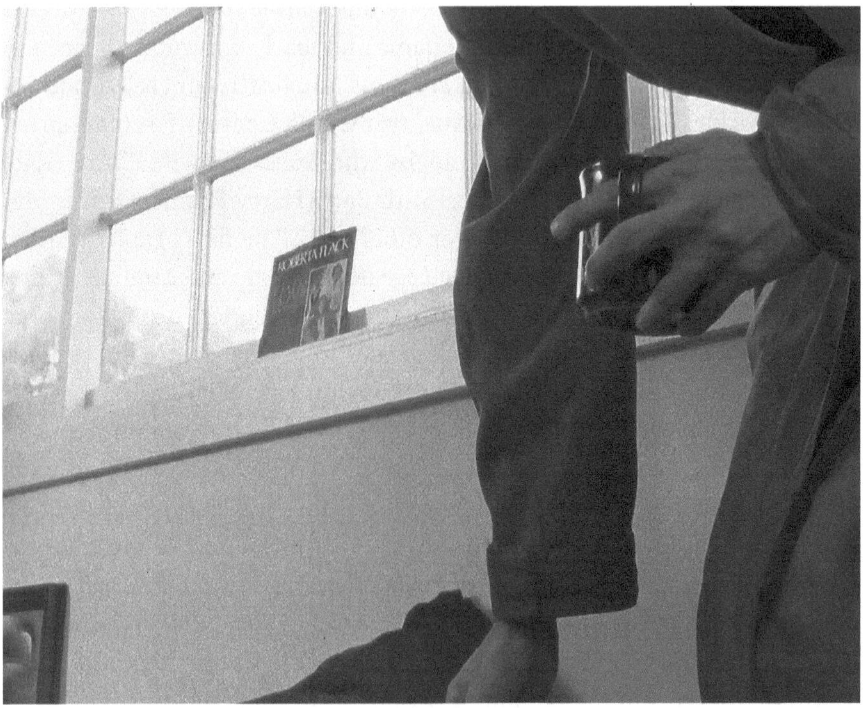

Figure 34
Jon's copy of the Roberta Flack single "Making Love" appears briefly on a windowsill.

created" (Howell 2015, 121). Simon Reynolds, in a short essay on industrial music, highlights the genre's associations with masculinity: "Industrial dance music is enthralled by the outer limits of human experience, and in particular with the extremes of male psychology: the outlaw, the survivalist, the terrorist, the serial killer, the dictator, the technocrat. Industrial's aura is supremely masculine. The key adjective is 'hard,' as in hard beats, hard living, hardcore" (Simon Reynolds 2024, 82). However, there is some variety in the industrial tracks that appear on the soundtrack of *The Living End*: not all of it is punishing, hard, macho. The genre initially links together Jon and Luke, even before they meet: Luke is listening to KMFDM on his headphones while he spray-paints "fuck the world"; the same band is playing in Jon's car as he leaves the doctor's office.

And yet industrial is also used to mark distinctions between the two characters – and it does so in gendered ways. As Howell notes, Luke tends to be associated with "harder-edged industrial" such as KMFDM, music "that shows the influence of garage, punk, and guitar-driven rock" and "whose violent soundscapes and samples highlight his tendency to act on his anger." Jon, on the other hand, has more of an affiliation with bands such as Coil, "experimental electronica of the industrial genre," which may be "suggestive of his alienated existence before Luke" (Howell 2015, 134–5). The industrial tracks that are linked with Luke have male vocals. In contrast, when female vocalists appear in the songs on the soundtrack, Jon is the one listening. This distinction articulates a clear masculine/feminine dichotomy between the two men: Luke as hard masculinity, Jon as soft; Luke the hustler connected to the open space of the road, Jon the journalist to a domestic world of words and insularity. When Jon is finally fully seduced over to Luke's rule-breaking ways – given a blowjob while he drives along the freeway by the ocean – KMFDM's "Naïve" plays, a song Howell suggests combines masculine and feminine components (Howell 2015, 136). Throughout *The Living End*, the industrial soundtrack provides rhythmic, propulsive, urgent, and often abrasive colour and affect. What is lacking is any stereotypically "gay" music – whether showtunes, disco, diva pop, or club bangers. As Jamie Sexton summarises: "At its broadest level, music in the film denotes untamed queer desires. Opposing stereotypes of gay taste, music in the film is indicative of a more aggressive and *transgressive* gay subculture" (Sexton 2022, 41, italics original).

Meaninglessness

In 2013, queer electropop group the Ballet (composed at the time of Greg Goldberg and Craig Willse) released its album *I Blame Society*. Not only was the name of the record inspired by Araki's film, but a sample of dialogue from *The Living End* appears before the song "Meaningless": Luke's "fuck work, fuck the system, fuck everything" philosophical manifesto that he shares with Jon over the breakfast table. It gives way to a bouncy, mid-tempo track whose narrator articulates his position outside of the heterosexual system of weddings, family, and religion. The musical register of the song – which is in a major key, each verse followed by a light, airy instrumental chorus with a melodic keyboard line – sits at odds with the expression of dissidence embodied in the lyrics. With its memorable, poppy tune and lack of danceable propulsion, the aural aesthetic of "Meaningless" has little in common with the industrial soundtrack that permeates Araki's film. Its words, however, articulate a political position of nonconformity that rhymes with some of industrial's imperatives.

As Goldberg recalls, he wrote the song before he had seen Araki's film, and it was Craig who later introduced him to *The Living End*,

> probably for its anti-assimilationist and liberatory queer cultural politics. My guess is that the monologue jumped out at me as related to the gist of the song, and I thought it would be useful as a pause in the music, and to frame the song for interpretation. "Meaningless" could be read as sarcastic, but my intention was to embrace meaninglessness as a condition of freedom from social institutions … to imagine that you could say "I guess my life is meaningless" and it would be a positive thing. (Goldberg 2024)

When asked about the industrial music used in *The Living End*, Goldberg admits that he has "a low tolerance for minor keys and discordance," preferring noise "mostly in the context of simple, melodic songs in major keys." "Meaningless" not only reveals the content and style of Araki's film as a source of inspiration for other queer artists, twenty-one years on from the film's release, but also wittily and angrily deploys pastiche and pop to articulate its subaltern politics in ways that rhyme with Araki's own tactics.

Coda

Gregg Araki followed *The Living End* with his "teenage apocalypse trilogy": *Totally F***ed Up* (1994), *The Doom Generation* (1995), and *Nowhere* (1997). As I acknowledged in this book's introduction, the making of the first of these was interleaved with his work on *The Living End*. Like *The Living End*, *Totally F***ed Up* is driven by a political imperative: it opens with a newspaper extract revealing "that 30 percent of teenagers who commit suicide are gay." The film is broken into "15 random celluloid fragments" and features six young characters – two lesbians, three gay boys, and one bisexual boy[1] – hanging out, shopping, having sex, and recording video confessionals (one of the gay boys, Steven, is toying with filmmaking). Godard remains a key influence and reference: not only are the lesbian couple, Michelle and Patricia, named after the two lead characters in *À bout de souffle* (1960), but Araki has described *Totally F***ed Up* as his take on *Masculin Féminin* (1966). The director interjects intertitles throughout *Totally F***ed Up* that comment on its narrative ("can this world really be as sad as it seems?") and quote song lyrics ("your screaming automatic pain," a line from the Jesus and Mary Chain song "Blues from a Gun"). *Totally F***ed Up* ends with Andy (James Duval, who appears in every film in the trilogy and has cameos in many other Araki projects) killing himself by drinking bleach.

With *The Doom Generation* and *Nowhere*, Araki began to tap into European funding sources, resulting in slightly bigger budgets. This allowed for larger production crews and enabled him to license songs by bands for which he could not previously have paid. *The Doom Generation* and *Nowhere* are both more surreal, anarchic, and violent than any of Araki's earlier films. In *The Doom Generation*, a convenience store clerk has his head blown off with a shotgun, the severed head continuing to make noise and spewing thick split-pea bile; at the film's conclusion, one of the lead characters has his genitalia amputated with a pair of garden shears. A reptilian alien appears in various locations in Los Angeles in *Nowhere*, and the film ends with a giant bug bursting out of the body of Montgomery (Nathan Bexton), the romantic crush of Dark (Duval). (It is scenes like this that led critic Nathan Lee to refer to Araki as the director who put the "ew" in New Queer Cinema [Goodsell 2023]). In *The Doom Generation* and *Nowhere*, the bloodletting and surreality of particular scenes in *The Living End* are accentuated, amped up.

With the second and third instalments of the loose trilogy, Araki solidified his characteristic visual and aural aesthetic. This had begun to take shape with *The Living End*, but now achieved full realisation: a bold, pop use of strong and saturated colour; hyperbolic language, liberally peppered with non-sequiturs and aphorisms; stylised set design, including murals, signage, and décor that matches or complements the characters' clothing and contains carefully selected pop culture ephemera; exaggerated costumes, wigs, and make-up. These stylings were paired with soundtracks on which shoegaze and dreampop predominate. All of these elements have remained largely consistent across the last thirty years of Araki's career – not that critics have always been enamoured of Araki's auteurist choices and thematic preoccupations. In an indicative critical review of the third teen trilogy film, Liese Spencer writes: "Art-directed to within an inch of its life, *Nowhere* could just as easily be retitled 'Nothing,' its failure to engage with any real emotion not so much a comment on air-headed youth as a symptom of it ... One wouldn't want hectoring, but there's a slightly troubling lack of analysis or depth here that similarly mars his earlier films" (Spencer 1998, 37). Alternative, positive perspectives have also been articulated: Robin Wood, for instance, praises the conclusion of *The Doom Generation* for its attempt to articulate a polymorphously perverse alternative to heterosexual monogamy, calling the film "one of the most radical statements in American cinema" (Wood 1998, 339).

Following *Splendor* (1999), which focuses on the shifting dynamics between a young woman and her two boyfriends who all share an apartment, and a pilot for an MTV series made in 2000 called *This Is How the World Ends* (which was not picked up), Araki had his most notable critical success with *Mysterious Skin* (2004). Based on the 1995 novel of the same name by Scott Heim – the first time that Araki had worked with someone else's source material – the narrative concerns two teenagers, Neil and Brian, and the different ways in which they come to terms with being sexually abused as young boys by their Little League coach. For this sombre tale, Araki deployed some of his familiar aesthetic components (bold colours; a shoegaze, electropop, and post-punk soundtrack), but reined in some of his more surreal and violent excesses. The film lacks a cathartic ending, with Neil stating, in voiceover, "I wished there was some way for us to go back and undo the past. But there wasn't." As I have noted elsewhere, the "ambivalent, downbeat ending" to *Mysterious Skin* "has a similar tone to the ending of *The Living End* and the three teen apocalypse films: the final shots of each depict lead characters who have experienced severe loss and pain, and face uncertain futures" (Davis 2011, 44).

In 2007, the same year that his stoner comedy *Smiley Face* was released, *The Living End*'s original 16 mm print was cleaned and digitised. It received new colour matching and sound remixing. The remastering process cost more than the original film's budget. The spruced-up version was shown at the Sundance Film Festival in January 2008, where Araki was venerated at a dinner for key New Queer Cinema figures alongside Tom Kalin, Christine Vachon, and others. *Edward II* was also screened. The following month, the new version of *The Living End* was shown at the Berlinale, in the "Panorama" sidebar.

Interviewed at Sundance, Araki described the film as "a time capsule of that period," and expressed surprise: "even by today's standards, some of it's pretty startling" (Smith 2008). In late April, Strand released the new version of the film on DVD. Araki highlighted the generational shift that had occurred since *The Living End* was made: "Young people today can't even imagine what it was like to be gay in the late '80s and early '90s, when people were dying every day all around you and it felt like a war zone" (Duralde 2008, 65). For Marcus Hu, the political urgency of the early 1990s had been lost: "It's been replaced with fighting for the right to marry; the LGBT community seems more concerned with having children ... We are more educated about AIDS and HIV, and an era of sexuality died with it. Gay life seems so much more complacent" (Duralde 2008, 65).

In 2010, *Kaboom*, which centres on the shenanigans of a group of college students and their exploration of a mysterious cult, was released, and in 2014, *White Bird in a Blizzard*, adapted from Laura Kasische's novel of the same name, premiered at Sundance before attaining limited theatrical release later that year. Since *White Bird*, Araki has worked in television, predominantly as a director-for-hire on episodes of serialised television (including *American Crime*, *Red Oaks*, *13 Reasons Why*, *Riverdale*, and *American Gigolo*). As he says of this work: "It's like being in film school. You try to make the best episode you can, but it's not your creation. You apply all your directing and filmmaking skills to your episode. You get to make a cool little mini movie. It's quick. Usually the episode takes 10 days to shoot. You edit for three, four days, and then you're done. As opposed to a movie, like *Doom Generation*, 28 years later I am still working on it. They're like kids, they never go away" (Siemsen 2023).

In 2019, Araki wrote a spec script for a television series called *Now Apocalypse* with Karley Sciortino, and passed it to producer Greg Jacobs, who he had worked with on *Red Oaks*. Jacobs showed it to Steven Soderbergh, and the two came on board as executive producers. Starz, the premium cable and satellite TV network, signed up for ten thirty-minute episodes. The narrative of the series focuses on a group of four twenty-something friends in

Los Angeles navigating sex, love, and careers. A second season almost happened: "[Starz] paid us to write the whole second season. They paid the cast their full salary for season two. We were scouting locations and doing prep. The executive who bought the show, who was our shepherd, got fired. It was one of those Hollywood stories … I haven't lost hope. I'm just looking for some benefactor to come in and save it" (Siemsen 2023). After the second season fell through, Araki returned to his director-for-hire work on other people's television shows.

In 2022, thirty years after the film made its debut in cinemas, *The Living End* was included in a programme of *Pioneers of Queer Cinema* organised by the UCLA Film and Television Archive in collaboration with IndieCollect and Outfest, financially supported by (amongst others) the Andy Warhol Foundation for the Visual Arts. The series featured thirty-three seminal titles, including *Desert Hearts*, *Mala Noche*, *Tongues Untied* (1989), and *Paris Is Burning* (1990). Ernest Hardy, in an essay written for its catalogue, links *The Living End* with *Parting Glances*, praising both for "eschew[ing] the milquetoast sentimentality of so many AIDS-themed films." He argues for the historical significance of both titles: "Each film in its own way complicated the ways people living with AIDS were depicted, and in doing so also complicated the act of eulogizing people who died from complications of AIDS. What neither film lets us forget is the enormous canvas of hostility and bigotry from both the US government and a depressingly large segment of its citizens against which battles against AIDS were fought" (Hardy 2022, 7). *The Living End* was shown in UCLA's Billy Wilder Theatre on 26 February 2022, along with two shorts: Tom Chomont's *Oblivion* (1969) and Sadie Benning's *If Every Girl Had a Diary* (1990). After the screening, Gus Van Sant interviewed Araki, Mike Dytri, Craig Gilmore, and Marcus Hu on stage. Contradicting his 2008 Sundance interview with Damon Smith, but perhaps reflecting his view of the film three decades on, Araki claimed that when he was remastering *The Living End* "it seemed almost tame to me – it was all like, 'what was the hubbub about?,' you know?" ("Pioneers" 2022). The *Pioneers of Queer Cinema* series subsequently toured across North America, with selections shown in cinemas including the Berkeley Art Museum and Pacific Film Archive, Wexner Center for the Arts in Columbus, Ohio, the Cinematheque in Vancouver, and Metrograph in New York. Through screenings associated with this series, *The Living End* was able to reach new audiences and to be revisited and reappraised by those already familiar with it.

Indeed, in recent years, Araki's wider oeuvre has been subject to a considerable amount of reappraisal. In 2024, the Criterion Collection released the teen trilogy as a remastered Blu-ray set. For the first time in a decade, Araki has been able to secure funding for a new feature film: *I Want Your Sex* (like *The Living End*, named after a song title) is, at time of writing in 2025, in post-production. For four decades, Araki has been committed to maintaining his independence as a filmmaker, always working with micro and low financing to achieve his visions. Though not always commercially successful, his films have developed devoted audiences and have attained substantive (sub)cultural cachet. *The Living End*, for all of its low-budget limitations, is a key root document for unlocking many of Araki's preoccupations (nihilism and anomie, rebellion and dissent, the political necessity of finding likeminded peers and allies, the knotty erotics of queer attraction) and an aesthetic signature (Californian linguistic tics, a rich colour palette, underground and indie music, a taste for cartoonish excess) that have persisted across his career. But it is also a vital register of its moment, a livid, sexy, barbed attempt to capture the peril and fury of queer life in the United States under the shadow of HIV and AIDS. The virus is still with us, and pandemics can strike at any time; *The Living End* may still have much to teach us.

Notes

Preface

1 Glyn Davis (2002; 2004). For the second edition of the first of these, I authored a completely overhauled essay on Araki (see Glyn Davis 2011). That piece begins to set the tone for this book.

Credits

1 In some versions of the cast list for *The Living End*, actor and filmmaker Paul Bartel is credited as "Twister Master." The published screenplay for the film includes a scene in which Darcy and Peter are at "one of those unbearable parties where everybody's trying a little too hard to be hip and have fun at the same time" (Araki 1994, 59). People are playing Twister, directed by a Twister Master. It is unclear whether this scene was ever shot. Bartel – who appeared in a number of films with Mary Woronov, the pair often cast as a couple – would have added an additional element of low-budget, independent kudos to *The Living End*.

Introduction

1 The film's associate producer, Andrea Sperling, provided Peter Broderick of *Filmmaker Magazine* with a full breakdown of every line of expenditure in the budget of *The Living End*, from the rental of lenses ($1,200) and the prop gun ($150) to the costs of particular services, such as a film to 3/4" videotape transfer ($350). See Broderick (1992/1993).

Chapter Two

1 The symbol was designed by six gay men who called themselves the Silence = Death Project.
2 The "Read My Lips" posters caused some dissent among ACT UP members. As Crimp and Rolston (1990, 53) note, "ACT UP women objected to the sexual difference marked by the two images – men aggressively kissing, women staring longingly into each other's eyes – because it reinforced the stereotype of desexualized lesbian desire compared with sexy gay male desire. When Gran Fury made T-shirts of the kiss-in images, they righted the imbalance by using a historical image of lesbians kissing."
3 For a short account of the challenges faced in getting the film financed and distributed, see Pierson (1996, 34–44).
4 For a comprehensive retrospective appraisal of the achievements of *Longtime Companion*, see Román (2006).
5 Tom Kalin, artist website, https://www.tomkalin.com/modern-architecture.
6 The script describes this clip: "The Five O'Clock News. Some horrific disaster reproduced in living video colour for the entertainment of the viewing audience" (Araki 1994, 11).
7 A similar position is articulated by one of the girl teens in *Totally*

*F***ed Up*: "It's government-sponsored genocide. Biological warfare. I mean, think about it: a deadly virus that's spread only through premarital sex and needle drugs? It's like a Born Again Nazi Republican wet dream come true."

Chapter Three

1 The film Luke is referring to is, of course, *Breathless* (1983), the US remake of Godard's *À bout de souffle*; the "French chick" is actress Valérie Kaprisky.
2 There is also a scene in the screenplay (not featured in the film) in which Jon, in his apartment, talks to Darcy on the phone. The description reads: "Jon is soaking in the white tub, wearing a Jean-Paul Belmondo-ish hat, getting soused on generic beer (the shot looks like an outtake from *Pierrot le Fou*)" (Araki 1994, 13).
3 The spelling of Bookwalter's first name differs across various sources: for other writers, he is DeVerne or Deverne. I have used the spelling that appears in his obituary in *The New York Times*, 31 July 1987.
4 A further, subtle nod: when Jon becomes sick, Luke buys him some Campbell's chicken noodle soup.
5 In the published screenplay (Araki 1994), they are watching *My Degeneration*.
6 As B. Ruby Rich notes, Araki "insists his films are explicitly linked" to his "alt music" tastes: as he puts it, "a lot of them are the Jesus and Mary Chain, in the sense that there's a kind of naïve romanticism at their heart, surrounded by chaos" (Rich 2013, 92).

Coda

1 "I think I'm bisexual," says Andy; "I mean, I've never porked a girl or anything but – if it came down to it – I think I could." For a sustained

exploration of Araki's engagement with bisexuality across his career, see Engelberg (2018).

References

Aaron, Michele. 2004. "New Queer Cinema: An Introduction." In *New Queer Cinema: A Critical Reader*, edited by Michele Aaron, 3–14. Edinburgh: Edinburgh University Press.

Anon. 1992. "The Living End." In *Sixteenth San Francisco International Lesbian and Gay Film Festival*, programme, 60.

Araki, Gregg. 1991. "The (Sorry) State of (Independent) Things." In *Moving the Image: Independent Asian Pacific American Media Arts*, edited by Russell Leong, 68–70. Los Angeles: UCLA Asian American Studies Centre.

Araki, Gregg. 1992. "Production Notes." *The Living End* press kit, Strand Releasing, n.p.

Araki, Gregg. 1994. *The Living End/Totally F***ed Up*. New York: William Morrow & Co.

Arroyo, José. 1993. "Death, Desire and Identity: The Political Unconscious of 'New Queer Cinema.'" In *Activating Theory: Lesbian, Gay, Bisexual Politics*, edited by Joseph Bristow and Angelia R. Wilson, 70–96. London: Lawrence and Wishart.

Atkinson, Michael. 1994. "Crossing the Frontiers." *Sight and Sound* 4 (1): 14–17.

Batrouney, Colin. 1993. "The Passion of Gregg Araki." *Outrage* 119 (April): 40–2, 67.

Becker, Edith, Michelle Citron, Julia Lesage, and B. Ruby Rich. 1981. "Lesbians and Film." *Jump Cut*, no. 24–5 (March): 17–21.

Benshoff, Harry M., and Sean Griffin. 2006. *Queer Images: A History of Gay and Lesbian Film in America*. Lanham, Maryland: Rowman & Littlefield.

Bollwinkel, Paul. 1988. "Three Bewildered People." In *Twelfth San Francisco International Lesbian and Gay Film Festival*, programme, 14.

Broderick, Peter. 1992/1993. "The ABC's of No-Budget Filmmaking." *Filmmaker Magazine*, winter. https://www.peterbroderick.com/writing/writing/abcsofnobudgetfilmmaking.html.

Broderick, Peter. 2002. "Ultra-Low Budget Moviemaking: The 2002 All Digital Model." *Filmmaker Magazine*, Fall. https://www.peterbroderick.com/writing/writing/ultralowbudgetmoviemaking.html.

Burston, Paul. 1995. *What Are You Looking At?* London: Cassell.

Butler, Judith. 1991. "Imitation and Gender Insubordination." In *Inside/Out: Lesbian Theories, Gay Theories*, edited by Diana Fuss, 13–31. London: Routledge.

"Cart." 1989. "The Long Weekend (O' Despair)" (review). *Variety*, 24–30 May: 34.

Chambers, Ross. 1997. "Reading, Mourning, and the Death of the Author." *Narrative* 5 (1): 67–76.

Chang, Chris. 1994. "Absorbing Alternative." *Film Comment* 30 (5): 47–53.

Chin, Daryl. 1993. "Girlfriend in a Coma: Notes on the Films of Gregg Araki." In *Queer Looks: Perspectives on Lesbian and Gay Film and Video*, edited by Martha Gever, John Greyson, and Pratibha Parmar, 103–7. London: Routledge.

Chua, Lawrence. 1992. "Gregg Araki." *BOMB* 41 (Fall): 26–8.

Creekmur, Corey K. 1997. "On the Run and on the Road: Fame and the Outlaw Couple in American Cinema." In *The Road Movie Book*, edited by Steven Cohan and Ina Rae Hark, 90–109. London: Routledge.

Crimp, Douglas with Adam Rolston. 1990. *AIDS Demo Graphics*. Seattle: Bay Press.

Davis, Glyn. 2002. "Gregg Araki." In *Fifty Contemporary Filmmakers*, edited by Yvonne Tasker, 25–33. London: Routledge.

Davis, Glyn. 2004. "Camp and Queer and the New Queer Director: Case Study – Gregg Araki." In *New Queer Cinema: A Critical Reader*, edited by Michele Aaron, 53–67. Edinburgh: Edinburgh University Press.

Davis, Glyn. 2011. "Gregg Araki." In *Fifty Contemporary Film Directors*, edited by Yvonne Tasker, 38–46. London: Routledge.

Davis, Steve. 1992. "The Living End" review. *Austin Chronicle*, 13 November. https://www.austinchronicle.com/events/film/1992-11-13/139356.

De Lauretis, Teresa. 1991. "Queer Theory: Lesbian and Gay Sexualities, an Introduction." *differences* 3 (2): iii–xviii.

Dry, Jude. 2022. "Gregg Araki Was 'Born at the Exact Right Moment' to Ignite '90s Queer Punk Rock Cinema." *Indiewire*, 17 August. https://www.indiewire.com/features/general/gregg-araki-punk-cinema-queer-90s-1234752647.

Duralde, Alonso. 2008. "*The Living End* Lives Again." *The Advocate*, 6 May: 65.

Dyer, Richard. 1977. "Stereotyping." In *Gays and Film*, edited by Richard Dyer, 27–39. London: BFI.

Dyer, Richard. 2002. "Introduction." In *The Culture of Queers*, 1–14. London: Routledge.

Dyer, Richard. 2003. *Now You See It: Studies on Lesbian and Gay Film*. London: Routledge, 2nd edition.

Dyer, Richard. 2007. *Pastiche*. London: Routledge.

"Edna." 1987. "Locarno Fest Reviews – Three Bewildered People in the Night." *Variety*, 19 August: 18.

Engelberg, Jacob. 2018. "'How Could Any One Relationship Ever Possibly Be Fulfilling?': Bisexuality, Nonmonogamy, and the Visualization of Desire in the Cinema of Gregg Araki." *Journal of Bisexuality* 18 (1): 102–17.

Finch, Mark. 1989. "The Long Weekend (O' Despair)." In *Thirteenth San Francisco International Lesbian and Gay Film Festival*, programme, 12.

Francke, Lizzie. 1993. "The Living End" (review). *Sight and Sound* 3 (2): 49–50.

Frino, Madeline. 2024. "Peaches' Playlist #2: Gregg Araki on…" *Peaches' Playlist*, Substack. https://peachesplaylist.substack.com/p/peaches-playlist-2-gregg-araki-on.

Galvin, Angela. 1994. "*Basic Instinct*: Damning Dykes." In *The Good, the Bad and the Gorgeous: Popular Culture's Romance with Lesbianism*, edited by Diane Hamer and Belinda Budge, 218–31. London: Pandora.

Gilbey, Ryan. 2020. "Todd Haynes: 'People Who Say Trump Is Bound to Win Are Letting It Happen.'" *Guardian*, 26 February. https://www.theguardian.com/film/2020/feb/26/todd-haynes-interview-dark-waters-dupont-pollution.

Goldberg, Greg. 2024. Email to author, 30 November.

Goldstein, Richard. 1990. "The Implicated and the Immune: Cultural Responses to AIDS." *Milbank Quarterly* 68: 295–319.

Goodsell, Luke. 2023. "Hush Puppies in Heat." *Metrograph*. https://metrograph.com/hush-puppies-in-heat/?v=7885444af42e.

"Gregg Araki Industry Talk." 2023. Sundance London, 19 August. https://www.youtube.com/watch?v=Mj_tp-d5SCQ.

Grundmann, Roy. 1990. "Longtime Companion." *Cineaste* 18 (1): 47–9.

Grierson, Tim, Sam Adams, David Fear, and Elisabeth Garber-Paul. 2021. "25 Greatest Punk Rock Movies of All Time." *Rolling Stone*, 20 April. https://www.rollingstone.com/tv-movies/tv-movie-lists/25-greatest-punk-rock-movies-of-all-time-103577.

Grundmann, Roy. 1993. "The Fantasies We Live By: Bad Boys in *Swoon* and *The Living End*." *Cineaste* 19 (4): 25–9.

Hall, Donald E. 2003. *Queer Theories*. Houndsmills, Basingstoke: Palgrave Macmillan.

Hanson, Ellis. 1999. "Introduction: Out Takes." In *Out Takes: Essays on Queer Theory and Film*, edited by Ellis Hanson, 1–19. Durham, NC: Duke University Press.

Hardy, Ernest. 2022. "We Get the Funniest Looks from Everyone We Meet." *Pioneers of Queer Cinema*, programme, 4–8.

Hart, Kylo-Patrick R. 2010. *Images for a Generation Doomed: The Films and Career of Gregg Araki*. Maryland: Lexington Books.

Hays, Matthew. 2007. *The View from Here: Conversations with Gay and Lesbian Filmmakers*. Vancouver: Arsenal Pulp Press.

Holden, Stephen. 1992. "A Film Series with an Eye for Offbeat Relationships." *New York Times*, 20 March: C1, C20.

Howell, Amanda. 2015. *Popular Film Music and Masculinity in Action: A Different Tune*. London: Routledge.

Jagose, Annamarie. 1996. *Queer Theory: An Introduction*. New York: New York University Press.

Jameson, Fredric. 1991. *Postmodernism, or the Cultural Logic of Late Capitalism*. London: Verso.

Jarman, Derek. 1992. Contribution to "Queer Questions." *Sight and Sound* 2 (5): 34–5.

Juhasz, Alexandra. 1995. *AIDS TV: Identity, Community, and Alternative Video*. Durham, NC: Duke University Press.

Kalin, Tom. 2004. Interview for ACT UP Oral History Project, 4 February. https://www.actuporalhistory.org/numerical-interviews/042-tom-kalin.

King, Geoff. 2005. *American Independent Cinema*. London: IB Tauris.

King-Clements, Eloise. 2023. "'You're a Freak, Too': Gregg Araki, in Conversation with Richard Linklater." *Interview*, 10 October. https://www.interviewmagazine.com/film/youre-a-freak-too-gregg-araki-in-conversation-with-richard-linklater.

Kleinhans, Chuck. 1998. "Independent Features: Hopes and Dreams." In *The New American Cinema*, edited by Jon Lewis, 307–27. Durham, NC: Duke University Press.

LaBruce, Bruce. 1995. "The Wild, Wild World of Fanzines: Notes from a Reluctant Pornographer." In *A Queer Romance: Lesbians, Gay Men and Popular Cultures*, edited by Paul Burston and Colin Richardson, 186–95. London: Routledge.

Laderman, David. 2002. *Driving Visions: Exploring the Road Movie*. Austin, TX: University of Texas Press.

Lally, Kevin. 1994. "Strand Thriving with Alternative Fare." *The Film Journal (Archive: 1979–1996)* 97 (10): 10, 59.

Lang, Robert. 1997. "*My Own Private Idaho* and the New Queer Road Movies." In *The Road Movie Book*, edited by Steven Cohan and Ina Rae Hark, 330–48. London: Routledge.

Lyons, Charles. 1997. *The New Censors: Movies and the Culture Wars*. Philadelphia: Temple University Press.

Maslin, Janet. 1992. "Review/Film Festival: *The Living End*; Footloose, Frenzied and HIV-Positive." *New York Times*, 3 April. https://www.nytimes.com/1992/04/03/movies/review-film-festival-the-living-end-footloose-frenzied-and-hiv-positive.html.

Mills, Katie. 1997. "Revitalizing the Road Genre: *The Living End* as an AIDS Road Film." In *The Road Movie Book*, edited by Steven Cohan and Ina Rae Hark, 307–29. London: Routledge.

Oishi, Eve. 2017. "Queer Experimental Asian American Media." In *The Routledge Companion to Asian American Media*, edited by Lori Kido Lopez and Vincent N. Pham, 107–18. London: Routledge.

Okada, Jun. 2015. *Making Asian American Film and Video: History, Institutions, Movements*. New Brunswick: Rutgers University Press.

Okewole, Seun. 1992. "Tom Kalin." *Sight and Sound* 2 (5): 36–7.

Ortner, Sherry. 2013. *Not Hollywood: Independent Film at the Twilight of the American Dream*. Durham, NC: Duke University Press.

Parmar, Pratibha. 1992. Contribution to "Queer Questions." *Sight and Sound* 2 (5): 35.

Pearl, Monica. 2004. "AIDS and New Queer Cinema." In *New Queer Cinema: A Critical Reader*, edited by Michele Aaron, 23–35. Edinburgh: Edinburgh University Press.

Pierson, John. 1996. *Spike, Mike, Slackers and Dykes: A Guided Tour Across a Decade of Independent American Cinema*. London: Faber and Faber.

"*Pioneers of Queer Cinema – The Living End*." 2022. UCLA Film and Television Archive, 26 February. https://www.youtube.com/watch?v=r4WGVA3ku0A.

Polan, Dana. 1993. *In a Lonely Place*. London: BFI.

Reynolds, Dale. 1993. "An In-Your-Face Kind of Director." *Gay Times* 172 (January): 32–4.

Reynolds, Simon. 2024. *Futuromania: Electronic Dreams, Desiring Machines and Tomorrow's Music Today*. London: White Rabbit.

Rich, B. Ruby. 1992. "New Queer Cinema." *Sight and Sound* 2 (5): 30–4.

Rich, B. Ruby. 1993. "Reflections on a Queer Screen." *GLQ* 1 (1): 83–91.

Rich, B. Ruby. 2000. "Queer and Present Danger." *Sight and Sound* 10 (3): 22–5.

Rich, B. Ruby. 2013. *New Queer Cinema: The Director's Cut*. Durham, NC: Duke University Press.

Ring, Trudy. 1992. "*The Living End*: Love and Hitchhiking in the Face of Death." *Outlines* 6 (3): 28, 40.

Román, David. 2006. "Remembering AIDS: A Reconsideration of the film *Longtime Companion*." *GLQ* 12 (2): 281–301.

Russo, Vito. 1987. *The Celluloid Closet: Homosexuality in the Movies*. London: Harper and Row, 2nd edition.

Schulman, Sarah. 2021. *Let the Record Show: A Political History of ACT UP New York, 1987–1993*. New York: Farrar, Straus and Giroux.

Sexton, Jamie. 2022. *Freak Scenes: American Indie Cinema and Indie Music Cultures*. Edinburgh: Edinburgh University Press.

Siemsen, Thora. 2023. "Gregg Araki in Conversation with Thora Siemsen." *Metrograph*. https://metrograph.com/gregg-araki/?v=7885444af42e.

Simkin, Stevie. 2013. *Basic Instinct*. London: Palgrave Macmillan.

Smith, Damon. 2008. "Rebel, Rebel: Gregg Araki Reflects on *The Living End* and His *Totally F***ed Up* Career at Sundance 2008." *Bright Lights Film Journal* 59 (February). http://www.brightlightsfilm.com/59/50arakiiv.html.

Smyth, Cherry. 1992. *Lesbians Talk Queer Notions*. London: Scarlet Press.

Spargo, Tamsin. 1999. *Foucault and Queer Theory*. Cambridge: Icon Books.

Spencer, Liese. 1998. "Teenage Kicks All Through the Night." *Sight and Sound* 8 (6): 36–7.

Sproull, Patrick. 2022. "Gregg Araki on 30 Years of The Living End." *i-D* magazine, 15 August. https://i-d.co/article/gregg-araki-living-end-interview.

Stimpson, Mansel. 1993. "In Your Face." *Capital Gay*, 12 February: 9.

Sturken, Marita. 2000. *Thelma and Louise*. London: BFI.

Taubin, Amy. 1992. "Beyond the Sons of Scorsese." *Sight and Sound* 2 (5): 37.

Tzioumakis, Yannis. 2006. *American Independent Cinema: An Introduction*. Edinburgh: Edinburgh University Press.

Waldman, Diane. 1990. "There's More to a Positive Image than Meets the Eye." In *Issues in Feminist Film Criticism*, edited by Patricia Erens, 13–18. Bloomington: Indiana University Press.

Warren, Steve. 1992. "Love and Negativity Among the Seropositives." *San Francisco Sentinel* 20 (35), 27 August: 25, 30.

Watney, Simon. 1987. "The Spectacle of AIDS." *October* 43 (Winter): 71–86.

Watney, Simon. 1991. "Outing." *Artforum* 30 (3): 16–18.

Watney, Simon. 1992. "Short-Term Companions: AIDS as Popular Entertainment." In *A Leap in the Dark: AIDS, Art and Contemporary Culture*, edited by Allan Klusacek and Ken Morrison, 152–66. Montreal: Véhicule.

Waugh, Thomas. 2000. *The Fruit Machine: Twenty Years of Writing on Queer Cinema*. Durham, NC: Duke University Press.

Waugh, Thomas. 2006. *The Romance of Transgression: Queering Sexualities, Nations, Cinemas*. Montreal and Kingston: McGill-Queen's University Press.

Whatling, Clare. 1997. *Screen Dreams: Fantasising Lesbians in Film*. Manchester: Manchester University Press.

Witt, Michael. 1999. "The Death(s) of Cinema According to Godard." *Screen* 40 (3): 331–46.

Wood, Robin. 1983. *Howard Hawks*. London: BFI, revised edition.

Wood, Robin. 1998. *Sexual Politics and Narrative Film: Hollywood and Beyond*. New York: Columbia University Press.

Wuest, Bryan. 2018. "A Shelf of One's Own: A Queer Production Studies Approach to LGBT Film Distribution and Categorization." *Journal of Film and Video* 70 (3–4): 24–43.

Wyatt, Justin. 1993. "Cinematic/Sexual Transgression: An Interview with Todd Haynes." *Film Quarterly* 46 (3): 2–8.

Wyatt, Justin. 1998. *Poison*. Trowbridge, Wiltshire: Flicks Books.

Yingling, Thomas E. 1997. *AIDS and the National Body*. Durham, NC: Duke University Press.

Yutani, Kimberly. 1994. "Gregg Araki and the Queer New Wave." *Amerasia Journal* 20 (1): 85–91.

Index

Queer Film Classics

Edited by Matthew Hays and Thomas Waugh

L'Homme blessé
Robert Payne

Boys Don't Cry
Chase Joynt and Morgan M Page

Orlando
Russell Sheaffer

Appropriate Behavior
Maria San Filippo

Midnight Cowboy
Jon Towlson

À tout prendre et *Il était une fois dans l'Est*
Julie Vaillancourt

Anders als die Andern
Ervin Malakaj

Maurice
David Greven

Winter Kept Us Warm
Chris Dupuis

The Children's Hour
Julia Erhart

Y Tu Mamá También
Juan Llamas-Rodriguez

Tomboy
Cristina Johnston

The Adventures of Priscilla, Queen of the Desert
Renée Middlemost

The Living End
Glyn Davis